THE
AMAZING
ADVENTURES
OF THE
JEWISH PEOPLE

THE AMAZING ADVENTURES OF THE JEWISH PEOPLE

by Max I. Dimont

Behrman House, Inc. • Publishers • New York

Dedicated to the teachers who steadfastly have
transmitted the Jewish heritage to Jewish youth

©Copyright 1984 by Max I. Dimont
Published by Behrman House, Inc., 1261 Broadway, New York, N.Y. 10001

Library of Congress Cataloging in Publication Data

Dimont, Max I.
   The amazing adventures of the Jewish people.

   Summary: Presents a history of the Jewish people throughout
the ages.
   1. Jews—History—Juvenile literature. [1. Jews—History]
I. Title.
DS109.9.D56 1984   909'.04924   84-16806
ISBN 0-87441-391-5

Designed by Gene Siegel

Manufactured in the United States of America

84 85 86 87 88   1 2 3 4

Photographs courtesy of:
Art Resource, page 20; Black Star, page 54.

Contents

Christian Europe protected by the Church and granted
unheard-of freedoms for the common man in feudal
Europe.

The Jews—after surviving the zeal of crusading Christians;
after resisting the temptations of the Renaissance; and after
having fortified their Judaism with the writings of a
quartet of great Talmudists—are herded into deadly ghettos with the coming of the Reformation.

The Jews—whose ideas until now have roamed the
universe—are stripped of their liberties and confined to the
cramped view of the world through ghetto windows, stage
three self-destructive revolts against their fate, and are at
last delivered from their hell by a Jewish hunchback and
a French emperor.

"Sixteenth-century" Jews, at last emancipated from their
three-century long ghetto imprisonment, march right into
the nineteenth-century enlightenment where, within one
generation, they become scientists, statesmen, and avant
garde intellectuals, but who yet believe that paradise, not
concentration camps, await them in the twentieth century.

Part III **Zionists to the Rescue (The Present)**
The Jews, who have poured into Palestine under the
impetus of Zionism, reach into the attic of their history to
arm themselves with the shield of David and the sword of
Bar Kochba to once again march under Jewish generals
giving commands in Hebrew to reestablish, against all
odds, a new Jewish state, the state of Israel.

A Note on Jewish Chronology

Jews begin dating events not with a king or a divinity but with the creation of man. In Judaism mankind, not a god or an individual, is the center of destiny.

Therefore Year 1 in Jewish chronology is the creation of Adam and Eve which, according to tradition, took place 3,760 years before the birth of Jesus, the event used by Western civilization as Year 1.

To find the Jewish date for an event occurring either before or after the birth of Jesus, just subtract or add the year in which the event took place from or to 3,760. Thus 1000 B.C. would be the Jewish year of 2760 (3,760 minus 1,000), and 1000 A.D. would be the Jewish year of 4760 (3,760 plus 1,000).

For practical purposes the Jews have adopted a common calendar with Western civilization. But instead of using the Christian designation of B.C. and A.D., the Jews use C.E. (Common Era) for A.D. and B.C.E. (before the Common Era) for B.C. So, for instance, instead of saying that the modern state of Israel was founded in 1948 A.D., or that David was crowned king of ancient Israel in 1000 B.C., the Jews say the former event took place in 1948 C.E. and the latter in 1000 B.C.E.

As scholars disagree on the exact dates of many events in Jewish history, some dates in this book may be slightly different from those given in other sources. Such discrepancies, however, in no way affect the validity of the event itself.

Chronology

World History	7500 to 2000 B.C.E.	Jewish History
Jericho, world's first city, founded. First pictographic writing. Egypt at height of cultural summit. Sargon I fuses Sumer and Akkad into world's first empire.		
Hammurabi founds first Babylonian (Chaldean) empire. Phoenicians invent alphabet. Hyksos invade Egypt; expelled after two centuries. Assyria rises to power. Tribes from northern India invade Grecian peninsula.	2000 to 1200 B.C.E.	Abraham introduces monotheism to the world. Age of Patriarchs. Joseph invites Jews to settle in Egypt; new pharaoh enslaves them. Exodus under leadership of Moses.
Greek and Trojan wars commence; Troy falls. Assyria extends her empire. Asiatic Etruscans invade Italian peninsula.	1200 to 900 B.C.E.	Jews receive Torah at Sinai. Joshua conquers Canaan. Two centuries of rule by Judges. First kingdom forged by kings Saul, David, and Solomon. Breakup of kingdom into Israel and Judah.
Rome founded. Age of Homer. Greek city-states founded; ascendance of Athens. Assyrians vanquish Babylonians.	900 to 500 B.C.E.	Reigns of the kingdoms of Israel and Judah. Prophets enter Jewish history. Assyrians destroy kingdom of Israel; end of Israelites. Babylonia destroys kingdom of Judah; the people exiled.
The golden centuries of classical Greece (500–300). Persians defeat Babylonians. Rise of Macedonia. Alexander the	500 to 100 B.C.E.	Persians defeat Babylonians; permit Jews to return to their homeland. Temple restored. Reforms by Ezra-Nehemia.

Great destroys Persian empire. Rise of the Seleucid and Ptolemaic kingdoms. Rome becomes dominant power.		Greeks become masters of Judah. Jews overthrow Seleucid rule, establish Hasmonean dynasty.
Rome invades Gaul, conquers Britain. Roman Republic dies as Caesars take over. Rule of Augustus, Nero, Vespasian, Titus. Two centuries of Roman persecution of Christians.	**100 B.C.E.** **to** **100 C.E.**	Rome annexes Hasmonean kingdom, establishes rule of procurators. Jesus born. Romans destroy Jerusalem and gut the Temple. Masada falls and Jews are exiled. Change over from priestly to rabbinic Judaism
Persians reappear as Sassanids, establish Sassanid empire. Emperor Constantine converts to Christianity. First barbarian invasions. Roman empire disintegrates	**100** **to** **600** **C.E.**	Bar Kochba stages new uprising against Rome. Judah Hanasi codifies the Mishna. Jewish history shifts from Roman to Sassanid empire. Abba Arika and Mar Samuel start the Gemara. Rav Ashi fuses Mishna and Gemara into the Talmud.
Mohammed is born. Islamic empire extended from India to the Atlantic. Spain invaded by Moors. Barbarian invasions of Europe continue. Charlemagne stabilizes Europe, founds Frankish empire.	**600** **to** **1100** **C.E.**	In the Islamic World: Jews come under Muslim rule. Age of the great Radanite merchants. Rule of the Talmud established. Revolt of the Karaites.
William the Conqueror invades Britain. Islamic empire begins to crumble.		In the Christian World: Jews survive barbarian invasions. Gershom convokes synod to solve survival problems. Rashi Europeanizes Babylonian Talmud.
Two centuries of Crusades followed by two centuries of the Renaissance. Heresies plague the church. Christians begin reconquest of Muslim Spain; expel the Moors. Protestant Reformation sweeps Europe. Century of religious wars. America discovered. End of feudal Europe.	**1100** **to** **1600** **C.E.**	First Crusade plays havoc with Jewish life. Jews enter Renaissance with great expectations. Two centuries of great European Talmudists. Sephardi culture clashes with Ashkenazi way of life. Spain and Portugal expel the Jews. Jews swept into ghettos in wake of Reformation.

Religious wars end with Treaty of Westphalia. Russia and Prussia emerge as new powers. French Revolution shakes Europe's ruling elite. Napoleon becomes emperor; reshapes Europe's political frontiers. Thirteen colonies founded. Revolution against England gives birth to the United States of America.

1600 to 1800 C.E.

Jews languish in ghettos and shtetls. Salon and court Jews make their debut in Jewish history. Heresies wrack Jewish ranks. Mendelssohn maps intellectual path out of ghetto; Napoleon paves political road to freedom. Jewish settlements grow in New World.

Democratic revolutions sweep Europe. Bismarck forges modern Germany. Romanov czars lead Russia to catastrophy. World War I shatters Europe's political framework—Russia goes communist; Italy goes fascist; Hitler rises to power, and world heads for World War II. China goes communist. Europe loses balance of power to United States and Russia.

1800 to present

Racism sweeps Jews into new frontiers of danger. Dreyfus Affair. Herzl founds political Zionism. Communist Russia threatens Jewish religion; Nazis murder six million Jews. America becomes largest Jewish Diaspora center. Zionism sweeps Jews on a tide of victory across two millenia of statelessness into statehood. Jews victorious in five Arab wars.

INTRODUCTION
The People That Would Not Die

On the face of a precipitous rock rising 1,700 feet into the sky, the scribes of Darius I, King of Persia, 2,500 years ago, chiseled this message:

"I am Darius, King of kings, King of Persia, King of Babylonia, Assyria, Arabia, Egypt. . . ." The inscription went on to list the twenty-three countries he had vanquished, and ended with this prediction:

"My empire will endure forever and ever."

Darius should never have gone into the prediction business. The Persian empire lasted only two hundred years. It was smashed by Alexander the Great of Macedonia.

Darius, however, had not invented the custom of predicting eternal life for one's own empire. There were many precedents. Two thousand years before him, another king, Sargon the Great, united the Akkadian and Sumerian city-states into the world's first empire (around 3,500 B.C.E.). Calling himself "King of Universal Dominion," he too predicted his empire would last forever. It lasted only a century and then was devastated by barbarian invaders. Other kings after Darius proclaimed the same message. But their empires, too, disintegrated.

Along with these empires, the people who had founded them

vanished also—the Hittites, Canaanites, Phoenicians, Assyrians, Babylonians, Persians, the ancient Egyptians, the ancient Greeks, the ancient Romans. Although the people who now live in the countires called Egypt and Greece still call themselves Egyptians and Greeks, they are so in name only. They are no longer the same ethnic people who had lived there in ancient times. They no longer have the same religion, the same language, or the same traditions.

There is, however, one exception. There still exists one people that lived at the same time as all these ancient empires, a people that still has the same religion, the same language, the same ethnic unity it had 4,000 years ago when it started out in history. This people is still as mentally alert and alive today as it was then, and yet more modern than ever. It is the Jews.

The Jews helped build cities in Egypt, witnessed the rise of the Assyrians to world dominance, beheld the resurgence of the Babylonians and the destruction of Nineveh. They were scribes and cupbearers to the kings of Persia. They were on hand to greet Alexander the Great when he passed through Jerusalem on his way to conquer the world. They saw the Greek civilization succumb to the legions of Rome, and stood at the bier of Julius Caesar.

Through the centuries, and against all odds, the Jews survived. They survived the fall of the Roman empire. They survived Muslim rule as mathematicians, poets, and scientists; they survived the feudal experience as scholars, businessmen, and ghetto tenants. And, after surviving the Modern Age as statesmen, avant-garde intellectuals and concentration camp victims, a small segment of the dispersed Jews returned, after a 2,000-year absence, to Palestine to reestablish the State of Israel.

Incredible, yet true.

Who are the Jews, and where did they come from? How were they able to survive where others perished? What gave them the ability to endure?

It was not survival for its own sake that guided Jewish history. Whereas the French philosopher Voltaire saw history as "little else than a picture of human crimes and misfortunes," the Jews invested history with a moral purpose. They were forever mindful of the warning in the Torah that "Where there is no vision, the people perish" (Proverbs 29:18). That vision was their life raft for survival.

The saga of the Jewish people is a fantastic adventure story. It is the story of a people in quest of the Promised Land. It is the biography of a people whose ideas conquered men's minds and toppled empires. It is the saga of a people that produced great warrior kings, prophets, messiahs, philosophers, and social reformers whose collective ideas influenced the world without making them its master.

To tell this 4,000-year story of triumph and grandeur, comedy and tragedy, as the Jews marched through four continents and six civilizations in four millennia, we will take advantage of many viewpoints. We will not, however, debate the merits and demerits of different religious interpretations, for all are equally valid in Jewish history.

THE FIRST ACT

The First 2,000 Years—
From Abraham to the Fall of Masada
(2000 B.C.E. to 100 C.E.)

*Moses, the dominating spirit in Jewish history, shaped
not only Jewish destiny but, with the Torah, embedded
the essence of ethics and morality into the consciousness of mankind.*

PART I

Adventures in Search of an Identity (2000–1000 B.C.E.)

The Jews begin their odyssey into history as nomads; wander in circles for centuries in search of greener pastures until enslaved by Egypt; are freed by Moses, given the Torah by God; and then, at last, head for the Promised Land of Canaan.

A three-century enslavement by Egypt threatened to put an early end to Jewish history. But the Jews survived to make another, more lasting, debut into history.

1

History Begins with the Semites

History begins with the first civilization which was sparked by a small segment of the human race known as Semites.

Who were these inventive Semites? When did they enter history, and how did they invent civilization? What is the relationship of the Jews to the Semites, and what segment of civilization did the Jews introduce to the world?

Archaeologists divide the people on earth into four main races, depending upon the color of their skin. The first is the Black, who mainly originated in Africa and Australia. The second is the Yellow, spread through the Asian continent. The third is the Red, native to the two American continents. The fourth is the White who, though originating mostly in northern India, now is mainly dispersed throughout Western civilization.

Each race is divided into language groupings. The white-skinned people are divided into two main language clusters, the Aryan (or Indo-European) and the Semitic. The Indo-Europeans, originally from Asia, speak such related languages as Greek, Latin, Spanish, German, English, and French.

The Semitic-speaking language group originated in the Near East, in a quadrangle bounded by the Tigris and Nile Rivers to the East and West, by the Mediterranean Sea in the North, and by the Indian Ocean in the South. It is to this group of people that the Jews belong, for Hebrew is a Semitic language. Other Semitic languages are Akkadian, Babylonian, Assyrian, Canaanite, Phoenician, and all Arab tongues.

Of all the races, it befell the Semites—the smallest segment of the White race—to usher in the first civilization. They provided mankind with the spark that transformed a two-legged beast into a civilized being.

It began ten thousand years ago in Jericho, around 7500 B.C.E., in Palestine, now part of modern Israel. Until recently, it was thought that history and civilization began around 3500 B.C.E. with the two city-states known as Sumer and Akkad, also part of the Semitic world. But archaeologists discovered through their excavations that the city of Jericho had existed for 4,000 years before Sumer and Akkad. Think of it—ten thousand years ago there was a city in Palestine that had paved streets, running water, houses of stone, and a protective wall around it. At that time in history, the people of Europe still lived in caves with wall-to-wall dirt floors, and drank human blood as a toast to their gods.

In the seven thousand years between the founding of Jericho and the establishment of Jerusalem as the capital of the first Jewish state proclaimed by King David, the Semites ushered in most of the innovations which history labels civilization. What were these innovations which changed the course of mankind?

Chief among the Semitic innovators were the Akkadians, the Babylonians, and the Assyrians. They created the first city-states, organized agriculture, and introduced the first unified governments ruled by written law. They developed the art of making linen, and learned to forge tools from bronze. They built the first sailing ships, built roads, and devised sanitation methods. They invented the wheel, tamed the horse, and controlled crops through complex irrigation systems.

These inventive Semites were the first scientists on earth, making great strides especially in mathematics and geometry. A thousand years before the Greeks, they knew the function of the square and the use of the root.

All these innovations—known collectively as the Bronze Age—comprised the first cultural revolution. The second cultural revolution, also introduced by the Semites, was the alphabet, which gave mankind its ability to write—to record the past and thus transmit that knowledge from one generation to another. Prior to the alphabet, the Egyptians, Assyrians, and Babylonians had been experimenting with various forms of hieroglyphic, cuneiform, and pictorial writing which culminated sometime between the eighteenth and fifteenth centuries B.C.E. with the Canaanite breakthrough of the alphabet.

The word "alphabet" was coined by the Greeks. It is a combination of the names given by the Semites to the first two letters, *aleph* and *beth*. The Greeks called them *alpha* and *beta* when they took the alphabet from the Phoenicians and adapted it to their own use.

Through the Greeks and the Romans, these Semitic ideas spread into Europe.

The Bronze Age and the concept of writing were the first two Semitic cultural revolutions. The third was a religious idea we know today as monotheism—the concept of one God of justice and mercy, an invisible, moral God who sets standards for mankind. This third cultural revolution was introduced by that segment of Semites known today as Jews, although they have also gone through history under such names as Hebrews and Israelites.

The introduction of monotheism by the Jews was a concept that shook the world and changed it. With monotheism, paganism was doomed. The Jewish idea of God took over, and new religions, new civilizations, new nations were born. The Jews, through their concept of God, gave history a new dimension.

2
A Handful of Hebrews

Jewish history begins inconspicuously when a Babylonian named Abraham appears and says "No" to the beliefs of the entire world as to the nature of God.

When the Bible introduces Abraham, he is not a Jew; he is a pagan. In fact, Adam and Eve, Cain and Abel, Noah and his sons—none are Jews. They are all pagans. Biblical narrative from the Creation to the Tower of Babel is a background for the entry of Abraham who became the first Jew in history after he left his native city of Ur to migrate to Haran, now a town in Turkey. There he had his first encounter with God. And there Judaism was born.

In those days, each nation had its own group of gods made of stone, clay, wood, or whatever material was handy. The gods had wives and children, and they were constantly at war. The people who worshipped these gods believed that they could appease them by buying expensive foods and sacrificing everything from animals to human beings to them. In turn, they believed the gods would insure them abundant crops, and bless them with victory in war. But these gods had no qualities of justice or mercy.

It was against this common belief about their stone and clay deities that Abraham rebelled. According to Jewish legend, Abraham's father was a wealthy merchant of idols. This legend relates that one day, when his father told him to tend store, Abraham smashed the idols. When his father returned and saw the havoc, he asked his son who was responsible. Abraham, pointing to the chief god, said "He did it." The angry father remonstrated that an idol of clay could not have done it. "In that case," asked Abraham, "how can that same idol protect us from evil or save us in war?"

In Abraham's encounter with God at Haran, God proposes a

covenant with him: If Abraham will follow God's commandments, God will make Abraham's descendants His people. God does not say they will be superior, merely that they will be His people and come under His protection. He also makes the promise that He will give them the land of Canaan. God does not say how long it will take, nor how it will come about. He does, however, stipulate one condition—all males must be circumcized.

Did this really happen? Or is it merely something Abraham perceived as having happened? From a historic viewpoint, it does not matter. What counts is that after four thousand years this idea still captures the Jewish imagination and shapes the destiny of the Jewish people. Though many things have changed in Judaism, the Covenant, the rite of circumcision, the Promised Land, are still central in the Jewish religion. If ever these concepts disappear, then the Jews will disappear with them. These perceptions have been the motivating forces in Jewish history and have continued to shape Jewish destiny.

Abraham's concept of monotheism was so revolutionary that it changed the behavior of the Jews more and more until they finally became a distinct group, with totally different thinking patterns from those of the pagans.

Because the God of Abraham has no ancestry, there are no mythological stories about His origin. Because the Jewish God is invisible, images of Him could not be made, and thus the Jews did away with idolatry. Because the Jewish God never dies, the Jews did away with the resurrection rites of the pagans. Because the Jewish God is spiritual, the Jews did away with all fertility rites and sexual orgies so common among the pagans. This moral conduct of the Jewish God set the conduct for the Jewish people.

And thus it was that the descendants of Abraham did not look upon themselves as mere nomads. They were the proud inheritors of a supreme God and the future inheritors of the Promised Land. History has rightfully called them patriarchs, for beneath their human frailty was dignity and purposiveness of action which would endure.

Four hundred years slip by. Abraham has passed the concept of one God to his son Isaac; Isaac bequeathed it to his son Jacob, the father of twelve sons, one of whom is called Joseph.

The time is now around 1600 B.C.E., and the floodlight of history is focused on Joseph whose brothers, out of jealousy, sell him to some Egyptians. In Egypt, Joseph becomes viceroy to the Pharaoh. A famine sweeps the land of Canaan where dwell Joseph's father and his brothers. Jacob sends his sons to Egypt to purchase some grain. Joseph reveals his identity to them, a reconciliation is effected, and a handful of Hebrews, who have roamed the land of Canaan, now settle in and around Egypt.

Unwittingly, Joseph has invited his brothers to disaster. A new pharaoh ascends the throne. Instead of viewing the industry of the Jews as a blessing for the Egyptian nation, this pharaoh perceives it as a threat and enslaves them. And thus, instead of being freemen, honored as equals, the Hebrews became indentured servants to the pharaoh, doomed to labor in brickyards and to build Egyptian cities.

Some historians contend that the Jews were swept into Egypt as early as 1750 B.C.E. as part of a horde of invading Semitic tribes known as the Hyksos, who defeated the Egyptians and enslaved them. After a two-century rule by the Hyksos, the Egyptians staged a successful revolution, and in turn enslaved the Jews.

Whichever version is correct, the fact remains that the Jews entered Egypt as freemen and ended up as slaves.

Then a totally unanticipated event took place. A hero named Moses appeared who rescued the Jewish people and catapulted them into the limelight of history again.

3
The Improbable Hero

The Bible wastes no words in introducing Moses. A new pharaoh has decreed that all male Hebrew infants should be killed to prevent the Jews from multiplying, and it is at this perilous time that Moses is born. When the danger of keeping the infant boy becomes too great, his mother places him in a waterproof basket to float down the Nile, in the hope that some kind Egyptian family will take compassion on the child and rear it.

By chance, it was a daughter of the pharaoh himself who found the child. She took the infant into the palace, named him Moses, and brought him up as an Egyptian prince.

As a young man, Moses found himself drawn to the Jewish slaves. One day, when he witnessed a taskmaster beat a slave, he slew the taskmaster and fled to Midian to escape the wrath of the Pharaoh. Here our future hero married the daughter of a Midianite priest, and for fifty years he tended the sheep of his father-in-law.

According to the Bible, God then appeared to Moses, commanding him to return to Egypt to liberate the Jews and lead them to Canaan, the land promised by God to Abraham.

Moses did not want the job. He was eighty years old, he was a stutterer, and he had no leadership experience. But after God alternatively threatened and cajoled him, Moses reluctantly accepted the mission. As a result, he became one of the greatest law-givers in history. He liberated the Jews, and after forty years of wanderings in the Sinai desert he led them to the frontier of the Promised Land.

Though the story of the Exodus is dramatic, it is eclipsed by another scene, the giving of the Torah, the Jewish "Magna Carta," to the Jewish people.

The concept of a written code of law was not a Greek, Roman, or

11

Christian innovation, but also a Semitic one. The earliest written code of law was developed in the city-states of Sumer and Akkad around 3500 B.C.E. This code was incorporated in the famed Code of Hammurabi (around 1800 B.C.E.). The Greeks had no written law until 700 B.C.E., after they had come in contact with the Semitic people who lived in Crete. The Egyptians, in spite of having been one of the earliest civilizations, had no written laws until 300 B.C.E.

The most villified concept in the Torah, often denounced as barbaric by scoffers of Judaism, is the law of "an eye for an eye, a tooth for a tooth," generally known by its Roman name, *lex talion*. The Jewish *lex talion* served to prevent punishment in excess of the crime committed. The offender could not be made to pay with his life for a lesser offense, such as causing the loss of an eye. This limitation of punishment led to the next step, that of paying compensation, not with an eye for an eye, but in money. Thus the Jewish concept of *lex talion* substituted public law for private vengeance.

The Torah also towered above all other codes of its day with its passion for justice and its demand for equality. The Mosaic Code asserted that man had a supreme right to personal liberty, and to private property. Accused individuals were presumed to be innocent until proven guilty; they had a right to call witnesses and to cross-examine their accusers. The accused could not be condemned to death except on the testimony of two witnesses, nor compelled to testify against himself.

In one bold stroke the Torah did away with class distinctions before the law. There was but one law for all—rich man, beggarman, king. In Babylonian law, if a nobleman killed a peasant he received but a slight fine; if, however, a peasant killed a nobleman, he received the death sentence, usually accompanied by torture. In Jewish law, murder was murder, no matter who committed it against whom. The punishment was the same for all offenders guilty of the same crime.

Even the rights of slaves were protected under the Torah. Kidnaping anyone into slavery was an offense punishable by death. Hebrew slaves had to be set free if they were abused. If a slave fled his owner because of ill treatment, he had to be set free. Compare this to the United States when, in 1857, the Supreme Court in its Dred Scott decision declared that a runaway slave was merely a piece of lost property that had to be returned to his owner.

It was not just questions of crime that the Torah was concerned with; it also created new frontiers of humanity. It forbade one to curse or mock the blind, deaf, and dumb, or to wrong a widow or a fatherless child.

Torah law even reached out to protect animals. Cruelty to animals was a punishable offense, and it was forbidden for a Jew to eat the meat of an animal who had died in pain. This led to the world's first humane slaughtering laws.

Three thousand years before today's environmentalists brought up the problem of ecological survival, the Torah protected nature from the depredations of man. The earth, said the Torah, is the Lord's, and man but a tenant who had to protect it from despoliation and safeguard it for coming generations.

Some Christian theologians say that the Torah is short on theology and long on legalisms. Thank God they are right. Though the Torah is a religious document, it is not concerned with the substance of God but with the conduct of man. The Torah contains a universal ethic for all mankind: Man, though created a little below the angels, still has to conduct himself on a plane far above the beast.

The first two festivals—the Sabbath and Passover—were also given to the Jews in the Sinai desert. The concept of the Sabbath has already been accepted by the civilized world, and Passover may yet become the world's first universal holiday. It is the first, and so far the only, festival in the world to celebrate the right of man to freedom from slavery.

Moses, the reluctant prophet, achieved his mission; he carried out God's intent brilliantly. For forty years the Jews had wandered in the desert, toward the Promised Land. In those forty years, the old generation died out and a new generation was born free. The Jews are now ready for a second entry into history.

Moses, who was eighty years old at the start of the Exodus, is 120 years old at its end. As the twelve tribes of Israel near the borders of Canaan, Moses dies. His death, however, does not take him out of history, but places him solidly in it.

What will happen next? The Jews are equipped with a covenant, and with the rite of circumcision. They have the Torah, the Sabbath, and Passover. They have a four-hundred-year experience as nomads, and a four-hundred-year experience in Egypt, much of it as slaves.

Are these laws, festivals, and experiences enough to sustain the Jews, to preserve them for the coming three thousand years?

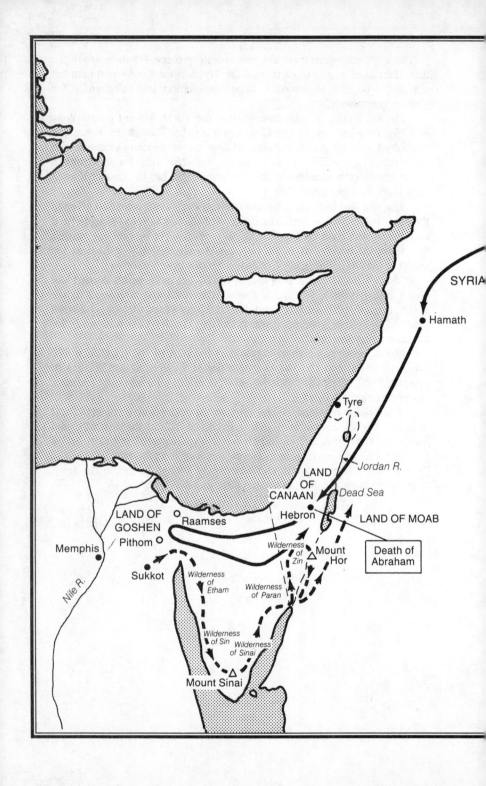

SYRIA

● Hamath

● Tyre

Jordan R.

LAND
OF
CANAAN

Dead Sea

LAND OF
GOSHEN   ○ Raamses

Hebron ●   LAND OF MOAB

Memphis ●   Pithom ○

*Wilderness
of Zin*

Death of
Abraham

Mount
Hor △

Sukkot ●   *Wilderness
of Etham*

*Wilderness
of Paran*

Nile R.

*Wilderness
of Sin*   *Wilderness
of Sinai*

Mount Sinai △

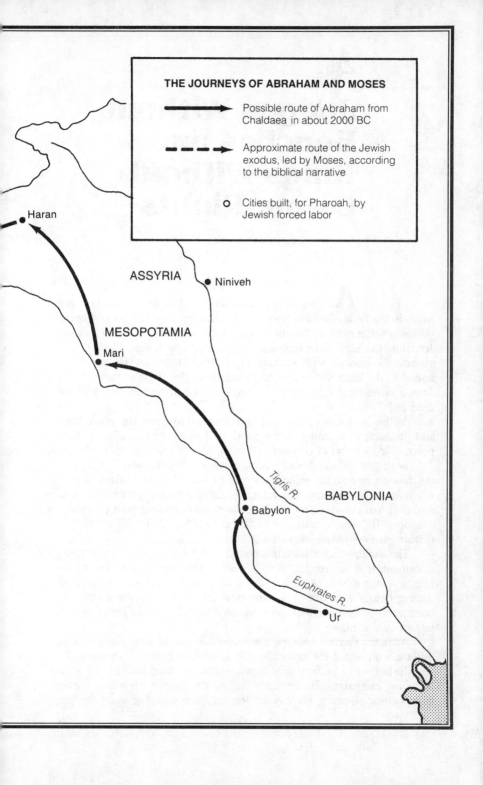

THE JOURNEYS OF ABRAHAM AND MOSES

Possible route of Abraham from Chaldaea in about 2000 BC

Approximate route of the Jewish exodus, led by Moses, according to the biblical narrative

O Cities built, for Pharoah, by Jewish forced labor

Haran

ASSYRIA   Niniveh

MESOPOTAMIA

Mari

Tigris R.

BABYLONIA

Babylon

Euphrates R.

Ur

4

Judges Without Benches and Kings Without Divine Rights

As long as the Jews wandered in the wilderness, they were, in the main, shielded from deadly enemies, involved only in minor skirmishes. But now, as they broke out of the wilderness into the plains of Jordan to the edge of the Promised Land, they faced danger. The land was abundantly stocked with Canaanites, Hittites, Jebusites, Philistines, all armed to the teeth and not about to surrender their land to these former Jewish slaves from Egypt who claimed that God had given them a divine deed to it.

As the Jews saw it, they had two choices—to forget the whole thing and go back to roaming in the Sinai wilderness, or to exchange their peaceful life for that of conquering heroes. They decided to fight.

With that choice, Jewish history changed. For the next 1,200 years, the Jew became an *ish milhama*, a man of war. He was destined to have magnificent victories and devastating defeats. But he always bounced back, sword in hand, spirit intact, ready to wrest new victories from impossible situations. He went to battle not to die but to win, and, like his adversaries, neither gave nor asked for mercy.

The Bible, which relates this period of Jewish history, is an amazing document. It is unswerving in its honesty. It does not hide human weakness or place a halo of perfection on its imperfect heroes. They are all human beings who often sin, who now and then have the decency to blush, and who sometimes even repent. The Bible is the first objective history ever written.

After the death of Moses, the leadership passed to a younger man, Joshua, who united the former Jewish slaves into a formidable army.

Joshua was a brilliant general who outmaneuvered his foes in a series of daring campaigns. He fearlessly crossed the Jordan River into enemy country, first storming the city of Jericho, then swinging north to stem

16

other enemy threats. As the Canaanites possessed chariots plated with metal and shields made of bronze, the Jews became guerilla fighters. They were masters of the swift raid and the deadly ambush, weakening the foe before engaging him in frontal assault or storming his cities "fortified up to heaven."

Canaan was defeated and rough boundaries were established for the first Jewish state. Joshua divided the people into a confederacy of twelve tribes, each tribe ruling itself. But above the leaders of the tribes, Joshua superimposed the authority of "Judges," who were mostly fearless warriors who against all odds vanquished an amazing and unending assortment of enemies. Though the names of all fifteen of these Judges have been preserved, three have captured the imagination of history—Deborah, Samson, and Samuel.

In addition to being a Judge, Deborah was also a prophetess, renowned for her beauty and bravery. As a Canaanite army under the command of the ruthless General Sisera marched against her, she appointed Barak as general in command of the Jewish forces. With ten thousand men, Barak climbed Mount Tabor and, at Deborah's orders, descended on the surprised Sisera. As Deborah had surmised, the previous day's heavy rains had flooded the valley, miring Sisera's dreaded chariots in mud. His army decimated, Sisera fled. He sought refuge in the rent of the beautiful Jael. But when Sisera fell asleep, Jael drove a spike through his temple, pinning him to the ground like a memo to a bulletin board.

The Bible relates that while Sisera lay dead in the tent of Jael, his mother peered out of the castle window worried why her son had not returned. Her maids comforted her by explaining that Sisera was busy dividing the spoils of victory, busy giving two Jewish maids to each of his warriors as reward for bravery.

Samson was an ignoble hero. Though legend has it that he killed lions with his bare hands and that he slew ten thousand Philistines with the jawbone of an ass, he actually made an ass of himself with his involvements with Philistine women. He was finally brought down by a Philistine beauty named Delilah. By giving Samson a haircut, Delilah emasculated his strength and brought on his downfall.

The last of the Judges was the Prophet Samuel who inherited chaos and anarchy in the land where, in the words of the Bible, "every man did that which was right in his own eyes." Even the people perceived this danger and begged Samuel to choose a king for them so that he "may judge us and go before us, and fight our battles."

Samuel's choice for king was Saul, a former farmer. With Saul's anointment as king, the Jews ushered in a revolutionary new concept of royalty—kings without divine rights.

The pagans regarded their kings as descendants of gods who were above the law. Not so with the Jews. The Jewish king had no connections in heaven. He was neither a son of a god, nor a relation to any god. No

NAZIR - Dedicated to GOD

divine origin was attributed to him. The Jewish king was as much subject to the law as an ordinary freeman or slave. Without formally labeling it as such, the Jews paved the way for the concept of constitutional monarchy, a concept the rest of the world was not ready to accept until the modern age when absolute monarchs were beheaded by their own people, thus putting an end to their lives and divine rights.

Tall, handsome, and moody, King Saul made a successful start. His reign was a succession of wars—chiefly against the Philistines. In one of them, Saul finally met defeat and, to avoid being captured alive, threw himself on his sword. The Philistines cut off his head and fastened the body to a wall. Saul's warriors, braving death, stormed the town and took the body down to give it a hero's burial. Saul's reign ended as it had begun—with the Philistines at the gate.

The age of the Judges had been two centuries of violence and war, two centuries in which the Torah had been all but forgotten in the struggle for survival.

The Jewish philosopher Abraham J. Heschel once defined a Jew as "a messenger of God who now and then forgets his message." In the same spirit, it could be said that the Jews are the keepers of the Torah who now and then forget they have it.

The stage was set for a king who would remember the Torah and anchor it permanently into the consciousness of the Jews.

PART II

The People with Two Countries

(1000–500 B.C.E.)

The Jews establish two small, hardy kingdoms
under the leadership of adventurous kings endowed
with *chutzpah* and charisma who successfully steer
their domains through peril-laden centuries until
finally vanquished by the two mightiest empires of
the day.

Not only has King David been enshrined in Jewish his-
tory as a great king but he has also captured the imag-
ination of Western civilization. This statue by Michel-
angelo encapsulates the grandeur and majesty of a
universal hero.

5

The Amazing Adventures of the Kingdom of Israel

Saul had not succeeded in unifying the twelve tribes. Upon his death, the nation was in chaos, and the Philistines were marching in the land. If Jewish history ever needed a little bit of luck, it needed it now.

That little bit of luck came from a most unexpected quarter, from someone no one would have bet on to succeed. His name was David, a sheepherder who in fairy-tale fashion had slain the giant, Goliath, and then married the king's daughter. King Saul's death put David, the son-in-law, on the throne (around 1000–960 B.C.E.). David seized history, bent it to his will, and inscribed his name in its pages.

David inherited king-size problems. Beset by enemies on every front, the new king threw diplomacy out the window and reached for the sword. In a succession of crafty campaigns, he set the Philistines reeling across the borders, dealt the Canaanites a death blow, wrested the city of Jerusalem from the Jebusites, and extended the boundaries of his realm from the Euphrates to the Gulf of Akaba. In so doing, King David forged a miniature Jewish empire.

Though David was a ruthless warrior-king, he has been enshrined in Jewish history for three more peaceful achievements—one political, one religious, and one literary. He so firmly established Jerusalem as the capital of Israel that it has been in the headlines of the world ever since; he so effectively anchored the Ark of the Covenant in Jerusalem that it became the holiest city in the land; and he penned most of the immortal Psalms which have become a literary heritage of mankind.

An incident in the life of King David illuminates how three thousand years before the rights of the common man were proclaimed in Western civilization, the common man in Israel dared challenge the Jewish king. King David, lusting for Bathsheba, the beautiful wife of one of his officers, sent the officer to his death in battle, then married Bathsheba. The point is not that King David acted like a petty tyrant, but that the Prophet Nathan denounced him publicly for this act. King David, despite all his power, did not dare to silence Nathan.

As long as King David was alive, his enemies, fearing him, were at his feet. The moment he died, they were at Israel's throat.

Solomon, the son of David and Bathsheba, who succeeded to the throne (960 B.C.E) through a harem intrigue, did not have the instinct for war that his father did. Though he lost to his enemies a sizable portion of the empire he had inherited, Solomon opted for peace. But to make sure there would be no further losses, he built a large standing army. Most famed of his garrisons was that at Megiddo, where he kept a reputed force of twelve thousand cavalry supported by some four thousand infantry chariots.* As no one now dared attack him, Solomon gained the reputation of being a king of peace.

With tranquility on his borders, Solomon set out to unify his country by breaking the power of the twelve rambunctious tribes. Trade and commerce thrived. As gold flowed into his coffers, he started an extravagant building program, including the Temple in Jerusalem which became a showplace of the ancient world. With pomp and ceremony, he enshrined the Ark of the Covenant in the Temple. However, one of the great mysteries of Jewish history is what happened to that Ark. It simply disappeared, and the Bible does not say when or how. It was not there when the Babylonians looted the Temple.

Though the country thrived economically, it began to show signs of a breakup. Idolatry found its way into the kingdom via King Solomon's bedroom. He had married an assortment of beautiful pagan maids, permitting each to practice her own religion. As his religious tolerance was not shared by the populace, his indulgence produced a civil war.

Even under King David, the realm had not had a strong centralized government. David's kingdom had consisted of ten tribes in the land of Israel in the North, and two tribes in the land of Judah in the South. Both King David and King Solomon had two coronations, one in Judah and one in Israel. But with the death of Solomon, the dual kingdom stitched together by David, was ripped apart at the seams. Judah and Israel declared their independence of each other. They anointed separate kings, and plunged into a civil war destined to last a century.

The subsequent kings in both Israel and Judah were colorful renaissance men of action. Against all odds, they kept the two kingdoms in the headlines for over two and three centuries respectively. With a bravery bordering on foolhardiness, the Jews in both kingdoms insouciantly stood up against the attacks and invasions of the mightiest of empires—Syria,

---

*The Bible gives three different accounts of his forces; modern archaeology disputes all three.

Egypt, Assyria, Babylonia. When other nations trembled at the approach of Assyrians or Babylonians, it was the Jews who rallied them to stand up and fight.

As Israel was the first kingdom to succumb, let us begin with her foray into history from independence to disaster.

One had to be a fearless individual to aspire to the throne of Israel, for it was a precarious post. The average life expectancy as king was only thirteen years. One king lasted only seven days. Few died in bed; most were victims of assassination. Altogether nine dynasties rose and fell during the 209-year rule of Israel (931–722 B.C.E.).

The first hundred years went badly for Israel. She did not have the strength to win, nor the will to end the civil war she had started with Judah. Then Israel had the luck to acquire a ruthless, capable king (880 B.C.E.) named Omri, who ended that civil war and decisively smashed a coalition of pagan armies invading Israel. Omri also built the city of Samaria, making it the capital of Israel. His success went to his head, and he decided on a few conquests of his own. He was successful beyond reasonable expectation, and his name was feared and respected by such powers as Assyria. Israel became known as the "land of Omri."

Omri's son and successor, Ahab, married a Sidonite princess named Jezebel. While her husband was out smiting the armies of Syria, Moab, and Tyre, Jezebel fanned the flames of religious hatred by introducing the worship of Baal and the sacrifice of children.

The time of Jezebel affords us another illustration of how deeply ingrained was the idea of life, liberty, and private property in Jewish law. King Ahab coveted the vineyard of his neighbor Naboth. But Naboth refused to sell his property. Jezebel, whose pagan mind had no room for such Jewish nonsense as individual rights, conspired to have Naboth executed so his property would go to the crown. But the Prophet Elijah dared speak out publicly. "In the place where dogs licked the blood of Naboth," he thundered at Ahab, "shall dogs lick your blood." People did not talk like this anywhere else in the world to kings without getting their heads chopped off until the eighteenth century when revolutions sweeping Europe gave the common man the rights which the Torah had given the Jews three millenia earlier.

Twelve years after the death of her husband Ahab in battle, Jezebel met a gruesome end. The Prophet Elisha anointed a general named Jehu, who murdered Jezebel and every family member of King Ahab. Having finished the purification task, Jehu proclaimed himself king of Israel. The cult of Baal was ended, civil rights restored, commerce invigorated.

Fifty years of peace ensued. But Israel become bored and went back on the conquest trail. With little effort she doubled her territory. As in the days of Omri, everyone feared Israel and left her alone. But Assyria, bent on expanding her empire, placed Israel on the top of her conquest agenda. Displaying her mighty army, Assyria held out the collection plate and said, pay tribute, or else. It was the age-old equation—your money or your life.

Israel became divided into two parties, one advocating that she pay tribute to Assyria, the other advocating no payment. When Israel stopped the payments, the Assyrian king, Tiglath Pileser, thought it was high time he taught the Israelites some manners—they were a bad example for docile, tribute-paying satellites. Leading a huge army, he marched against Israel.

But Israel was no pushover. It took the Assyrians ten years and three kings to subdue Israel, which finally fell (722 B.C.E.) after a three-year siege of its capital, Samaria. To make sure that Assyria would never again have to face such a formidable foe, the Assyrian king, Sargon II, deported a major segment of Israel's population.

It was a good thing there was another Jewish kingdom left, for Israel never recovered from that war. The Jews of Israel vanished into the vastness of defeat.

The very existence of the Jewish people was at stake. Of the original twelve tribes, only two were now left in Judah. Would these remaining two tribes be able to hold out against the enemy, where the ten tribes of Israel had not?

6

The Incredible Rise and Fall of the Kingdom of Judah

The throne of the kingdom of Judah was safer to occupy than that of Israel, but not much. In the 345 years of its existence (931–586 B.C.E.), the average occupancy of twenty kings was a little over seventeen years. However, in spite of frequent assassinations and intrigues, the kingdom of Judah had but one royal dynasty for over three centuries—all its rulers being direct descendants of King David.

Judah, like Israel, took to the sword and at various times won and lost Arabian, Moabite, and Philistine territory. For a century, she was blessed mostly with victories until a string of defeats reduced her to her former size.

The Jezebel story had its counterpart in Judah. Jezebel's ravishing daughter Athalia married Jehoram, the king of Judah. Like her mother, Athalia also encouraged the worship of Baal and Astarte. Upon the king's death, she seized the throne and ordered every member of the royal house of David killed. Only one member escaped this murder spree, her grandson Jehoash, who was spirited away. Six years later, Athalia was put to a gruesome death and Jehoash was crowned king at the age of seven.

Judah had managed to stay out of Israel's war with Assyria. But, whereas Judah was willing to leave Assyria alone, Assyria was not willing to leave Judah in peace. She held out her collection plate with the usual admonition—pay or be invaded. The king of Judah took one look at the devastation Assyria had wrought in Israel, and quickly signed on the dotted line.

The century from 722 to 622 B.C.E. was not a happy one for the kingdom of Judah. There was the Assyrian threat to be sure, but Judah was also plagued with internal troubles. The rich were oppressing the poor; the Jewish religion was riddled with pagan cults, and idols were reappearing in the bazaars of Judah. A century after the defeat of Israel,

27

the challenge facing the Jews of Judah was whether they could survive as Jews.

In her hour of need, Judah had the good fortune to inherit a hard-driving, resourceful king named Josiah (638 B.C.E.). Viewing the plight of his people, Josiah decided the nation needed religious and social shock therapy to cure its ills.

As King Josiah perceived it, he was not in danger of losing his country, but was in danger of losing the Jews as Jews. Blind luck came to his aid. During a renovation of the Temple, a momentous discovery was made. Hidden in a long-forgotten niche, a Torah document was found which Josiah proclaimed was the original Five Books of Moses. Some scholars contend it was only one of the Five Books, the Book of Deuteronomy.

But whether one or five, a religious reawakening swept the country. On the crest of this emotional wave, Josiah purged the land of sorcerers and necromancers, sent the pagan priests away and the worshippers of Baal and Astarte after them. Then he rammed through a series of social and economic reforms. After an illustrious reign of thirty years, King Josiah died in a battle against the Egyptians.

But the days of Judah were numbered. A new danger had arisen, the Babylonians, who were now on the march toward empire. Having destroyed the Assyrian capital of Nineveh (605 B.C.E.), the Babylonians annihilated the Assyrians at the battle of Carchemish. Now it was the Babylonians who held out the collection plate. After paying tribute for three years, Judah suddenly refused to continue.

An enraged Nebuchadnezzar, king of Babylon, personally led his armies to teach the stubborn Jews a lesson. To his consternation it was to take three wars and sixteen years to finally subdue Judah.

The first Babylonian-Jerusalem war came to a swift end. After a three-month siege, Jerusalem capitulated. The Temple was plundered, eighteen thousand of Jerusalem's finest familes were sent into exile, and Zedekiah was appointed puppet king.

Hardly had the Babylonians withdrawn than Zedekiah aligned himself with the Egyptians. Nebuchadnezzar made an about-face and marched against the Egyptians, who caved in without a fight while the Jews held out for a year-and-a-half. Finally, in the fateful year of 586 B.C.E., the Babylonians again breached the walls of Jerusalem and this time decided on a program of total devastation. The sons of King Zedekiah were slain before his eyes and then his own eyes were torn out. The city was looted and burned, the Temple destroyed, and all who were not sick or poor or crippled were deported.

But the Babylonians had again underestimated the Jews. The poor, the sick, and the crippled whom the Babylonians had spared, rebelled a third time and slew the Babylonian-appointed governor. But his third rebellion had been undertaken more in the spirit of defiance than in the belief of victory. After three Babylonian wars, the kingdom of Judah was finished.

The second half of the dual kingdom of King David and King Solomon had come to an end. Was this also to be the end of the Jewish people?

7

The Voice of the Prophets

Abraham gave the Jews monotheism. Moses gave them the Torah. Joshua led them to the Promised Land. King David established the first Jewish state and King Solomon built the Temple. The kingdoms of Israel and Judah persevered for more centuries than most ancient kingdoms. Had it all been for naught?

Dispersed in the vast reaches of the Assyrian empire, most of the Jews of the kingdom of Israel had disappeared into slavemarkets and through assimilation. And now the Jews of the kingdom of Judah, the last remnants of the Jewish people, trudged along that same captivity road to Babylon. Were they, too, destined to disappear like the Jews of the kingdom of Israel?

With hindsight of history, we know the answer. They did not disappear. They survived. But how? Why did the Jews of Israel vanish, whereas the Jews of Judah did not?

There is a Jewish saying that before God sends a calamity to the Jews he first provides them with a remedy. This time the remedy for the threat of Jewish survival was the Prophets.

The Prophets have a unique place in Jewish history. The Jews viewed them as men sent by God to show man the path to righteousness.

Subtly, the Prophets changed the future course of Judaism. They appeared precisely at the time when they were most needed to save the Jews. Even before the walls of Israel were stormed by the Assyrians, the voices of the first two major Prophets—Amos and Moses—were heard in Israel, but their voices went unheeded.

After the fall of Israel (722 B.C.E.), the center stage of prophecy shifted to Judah, where were heard the messages of a succession of new major Prophets—Isaiah, Jeremiah, Zecheriah, Micah. At first their messages did not seem pertinent. It would take two centuries for their words to germinate in the minds of the people who at first had been reluctant to accept them.

What did the Prophets preach that was to become so important to the future survival of the Jews?

In the thousand years from the days when King Solomon built the first Temple in Jerusalem to the destruction of the second Temple by the Romans, the Jewish religion expressed itself mainly in the sacrifice of animals under the supervision of priests. The Prophets, on the other hand, maintained that God abhorred vain sacrifices, that justice and mercy were superior to sacrifice and priestly ritual. God, said the Prophets, wanted higher ethical and moral standards from all human beings, not just from the Jews.

Those were daring ideas, and it is amazing that no Prophet was put to death by the Jews for uttering such heretic notions. What would have happened, for instance, to a Christian cardinal if, during the Middle Ages, he had dared to preach that God did not want confessions and Mass? Such a cardinal would have been burned, or flayed alive, as were Huss and Savonarola and thousands upon thousands of other Christians who were martyred for daring to oppose church doctrine.

But the Prophets also had a second message that was to affect Jewish destiny. They taught that God was not an exclusive Jewish possession, but was for all mankind. The Jews, said the Prophets, were the messengers of God, whose mission it was to take these ethical and moral values of the Torah to the world.

The Book of Jonah illustrates that command in a unique manner. God orders Jonah to go to Nineveh, the sinful capital of the Assyrians, to preach the word of God to the pagans. But Jonah ignores God's command and takes off in a different direction. A big fish swallows Jonah and disgorges him on the shores of Nineveh. In the way Moses was the reluctant Prophet, so Jonah was the reluctant messenger. But in the end both did carry out their missions. So that the Jews won't forget this message, the Book of Jonah is read in synagogues every Yom Kippur the world over.

From the idea that the Jews must be an example for the world, grew the concept that the physical commandments of God were for Jews only, and the spiritual and moral message of Judaism was for all mankind. This is the reason why the Christians, when they split off from Judaism at the end of the first century C.E., attached to their New Testament the original Jewish Bible. And this is why Western civilization is called Judeo-Christian.

With the Prophets, Judaism acquired a universal dimension. Judaism, which had started out as the sole property of one man, Abraham, was enlarged to include his family, expanded to the Twelve Tribes, nurtured into a nation. And now it was given its universal dimension by the Prophets. The Jewish religion became an exportable commodity, to be carried in one's heart and mind rather than tied to the Temple in Jerusalem.

The words of the Prophets were also to have a practical application in the Babylonian captivity. It was here that their words assumed a new meaning, giving the exiled Jews of Judah a blueprint for survival.

PART III

In Quest of Lost Jerusalem

(500 B.C.E.–100 C.E.)

The Jews—after establishing a thriving society in the Babylonian exile, after being given the freedom to return to Jerusalem by the Persians, after being flung into the Greek orbit of history, and after establishing a new, independent kingdom under the Hasmoneans—are first conquered by the Romans and then exiled by them as a punishment for not being docile satellites.

Masada, a steep brown rock shaped like a space-ship and rising 1,200 feet toward the sky, has become a symbol of Jewish resistance to the challenges of history. Here, Israeli paratroopers take an oath never to surrender.

8

The Priest and the Aristocrat

If you, the reader, were a member of a planning board whose task it was to draft a program to prevent the Jews of Judah from disappearing in exile, you would have to foresee four unanticipated and improbable events: The Jews fell in love with life in Babylon; the Babylonians were annihilated by the Persians; the Persian conqueror told the Jews, "Go back to Jerusalem"; and the Jews said, "No, thank you. We like it here."

Those Jews who "wept by the rivers of Babylon" were but a handful of zealots. The rest never had it so good. Instead of hating Babylonia, they loved it; instead of being reduced to pauperism, they became cosmopolitan citizens; and instead of wanting to return to Jerusalem, they established a thriving community in Babylonia.

Babylonian trade routes had taken the Jews to every corner of the then-civilized world. Their love of learning and adventure lofted them to high posts of commerce, scholarship and the professions. Far from being oppressors, the Babylonians were tolerant Semites who prescribed the philosophy of live and let live.

Nevertheless, the past had left its impact on the Babylonian Jews. The Torah had been implanted like a pacemaker in their hearts. Though they did not hop on the wagons for return trips to Jerusalem, they did want to remain Jews.

But how could they? The Judaism of those days—priestly Judaism—permitted sacrifice only in the Temple in Jerusalem. Therefore, exiled Jews could not practice it. The Jews of the kingdom of Israel, who had been exiled by the Assyrians a century previously, had found no answer to this dilemma, and they vanished from history.

But the Jews of the kingdom of Judah, exiled to Babylonia, did come up with a workable response, and they survived. Babylonia was turned into an experimental setting for new ways of expressing one's ties to Judaism.

The Babylonian Jews reassessed the words of the Prophets and innovated three new concepts. Because they were forbidden to build a temple for sacrifice on foreign soil, they built synagogues for religious assembly. Instead of offering animal sacrifices to God, they offered prayers. And instead of developing a new priesthood, they gradually initiated a new type of spiritual leader—the future rabbi.

With these innovations, the Judaism of priest, Temple, and sacrifice was supplanted and destined to disappear. Unwittingly, the Jews had sown the seeds for a new Judaism of rabbi, synagogue, and prayer, a form of Judaism still with us today.

There were universal consequences to these innovations. The synagogue became a prototype for the church of the Christians and the mosque of the Moslems; prayer became the universal symbol of devotion to God.

Through synagogue and prayer, the Jewish religion was no longer tied to the soil of Jerusalem. The Jews could build their synagogues in any land and eventually say their prayers in any language. The Jewish religion could now be carried in one's heart to any country. Survival for Jews in exile had been assured.

The second, totally unanticipated event was that the Babylonians, who had worked so hard fighting their way to the summit of power, had only fifty years in which to enjoy the fruits of their plunder. Five decades after they had destroyed Jerusalem, the Babylonians were annihilated by Cyrus, leading a new people (the Persians), belonging to a new race (the Indo-Europeans), and forging a new world power—the Persian empire.

If there is one thing history teaches us it is never to snub anyone on your way up, for you never know whom you will meet on your way down. For several thousand years the Semitic people had been the cultural and military overloards of the world, innovators of the Bronze Age, masters of agriculture, leaders in science, developers of writing. Now the luck of the Semites was running out as the Indo-Europeans took over. For the next two centuries the Persians were destined to dominate the world until another Indo-European people—the Greeks—would do unto the Persians what the Persians had done unto the Babylonians.

Who were the Persians? As early as 2000 B.C.E., migratory tribes known as Aryans (or Indo-Europeans), living in northern India, invaded the Mesopotamian basin. Here they flourished in obscurity for centuries, until a leader named Cyrus came along who unified them into a nation determined to make it to the top. The first major march in quest of power took place in 536 B.C.E., when Cyrus vanquished Babylonia and established his empire in the heartland of former Babylonian country. This shift of political power removed the Jews from the world of the Semites into the sphere of the Indo-Europeans.

Cyrus, a most enlightened ruler, viewed all religions as equally true and equally useful, including that of the Jews who worshipped an invisible God. This led to the third surprise; Cyrus announced that all people exiled by the Babylonians, including the Jews, were free to return to their respective former countries if they still existed.

The fourth surprise was that all Jews did not greet the edict of Cyrus with shouts of joy. In fact, it created mixed emotions. Why go back to Judah, where only poverty and hard labor awaited them?

(History has a penchant for repeating itself. The situation in Persia in 536 B.C.E. was very much like a situation in modern times. In the 1950s, David Ben-Gurion, Prime Minister of Israel, invited all Jews everywhere to return and settle in the new state of Israel. Like the Jews in the Persian empire, very few American Jews heeded that call.)

Jewish leaders now foresaw a new danger—that Jerusalem might cease to exist. And, if that were to happen, there would then be no cohesive ideology to hold the Jews in the Jewish orbit.

The Jewish leaders brooded upon this dilemma, obsessed with the idea that there must be a return to Zion, an idea which had been implanted in their minds by the Prophet Isaiah. Isaiah had forecast both the defeat and exile of the Jews of Judah, but had also prophesied a future return to their former homeland. Once the prophecy of exile was fulfilled, the Jews now in exile were encouraged that the prophecy of a return would also be fulfilled.

Firmly believing that God helps those who help themselves, the Jewish "planning committee" in exile came up with a startling recommendation. If the exiled Jews did not want to go back to Judah to till the soil of an occupied country, why not change the emphasis? Why not motivate them to return in order to lay the foundation for a future independent Jewish state? Why not become Zionists?

Of course, they did not call themselves "Zionists." The word "Zionism" was not coined until 2,500 years later when the Jews in the late nineteenth century C.E. began planning their return to Zion. But, like the latter-day Zionists in Europe, the "proto-Zionists" of Persia, figuratively took up the cry "back to Zion," and launched two "Zionades." The immediate aim was to resettle Judah and rebuild Jerusalem; the long-range aim was to restore the independent state of Judah.

The leaders of these two Zionades represented a new breed of Jews. The Patriarchs had been nomadic Jews; Moses and Joshua represented slavery Jews; the Judges and Kings were nationalist Jews living in a homeland of their own. The Zionade leaders, however, were the first Diaspora Jews, born and raised in lands outside their former national homeland, yet still retaining their Jewish identity.

The first Zionade, launched in 538 B.C.E., had a distinguished leadership—two princes of the house of David, Shezbazzar and Zerubbabel, who each secretly wanted to be king, and a pretender high priest named Jeshua. Their followers, however, were undistinguished, composed mainly of zealots without property, the poor without hope, and the ne'er-do-wells without either hope or property.

Nevertheless, zeal was there. Under the leadership fo this august triumvirate, the Temple was rebuilt and dedicated in 515 B.C.E. The formal opening was a gala affair. Sacrificed for the occasion were one hundred bulls, six hundred small cattle, and twelve he-goats to symbolize the twelve tribes.

Suddenly, Shezbazzar and Zerubbabel disappear. Some scholars surmise they were beheaded by the Persians who suspected them of having ambitions to set up an independent state. But since the Persians did not oppose the rule of a priest, a crown of silver and gold was placed on the head of Jeshua when he was anointed high priest. This event was of great significance. It gave the Jews a form of self-rule which could be expanded into future independence.

With the death of Jeshua, the wind went out of the first Zionade. In the century between the first and second Zionades, the *aliyah* from the Persian empire to Judah dwindled to a trickle. Again, speaking in modern terminology, the Jewish Diaspora leadership held another emergency session. Without Zion as a magnet in Jewish identity, there was again the danger of the Jews being hurled out of history. New leaders appeared to head a second Zionade—a priest named Ezra and an aristocrat named Nehemiah.

The Bible tells us Ezra was a scribe in the court of the Persian king. Many Jews view him as a second Moses, because he restored the Torah to preeminence in Jewish life. Though it was not an impressive Zionade numerically—a total of 1,700 souls—it succeeded where the first one had failed.

In Jerusalem, Ezra was joined by Nehemiah, who was a cupbearer to the king, testifying to the high positions Jews held in the Persian empire. The king appointed Nehemiah governor of Jerusalem, and here he joined Ezra in forging a remarkable program for survival.

As governor, Nehemiah's first concern was the physical survival of the Jews against attacks by unforeseen enemies. He felt that the walls around Jerusalem, which had been destroyed by the Babylonians, should be restored. Like the song during World War II advising the American soldiers to "Praise the Lord and pass the ammunition," Nehemiah advised the Jews to rebuild the walls around Jerusalem with a trowel in one hand and a sword in the other.

The enemy, however, was not without, but within. The danger was the disintegration of Judaism through the inroads of paganism and lack of knowledge of the Torah. To counteract these threats, Ezra and Nehemiah introduced two new ideas.

A ban on intermarriage was the first, and it stunned the Jews. This ban was totally different from the ban in the Torah which only prohibited intermarriage to Gentiles who had lived in Palestine prior to its conquest by the Jews (Deuteronomy 7:1–3). The Ezra-Nehemiah ban was established, not on any notion of superiority or racism but merely to prevent the dilution of the small number of Jewish people. It was accepted, however, as a practical solution to a vexing problem, the price to be paid if the Jews wanted to continue in history as a Jewish people.

The second step taken by this team was to expand the Bible which at that time officially contained only the Book of Deuteronomy. To it, some scholars contend, Ezra and Nehemiah added the four other books of Moses—Genesis, Exodus, Leviticus, and Numbers. From that time on, no changes, additions, or deletions were permitted, which is why the Bible to this day is remarkably the same as it was then. Ezra and Nehemiah also affirmed and reinforced the practice that a segment of the Torah must be read in synagogues all over the world every Sabbath and twice during the week.

We can now perceive a thread of destiny in Jewish history. We see it unfold like a vast drama, in a succession of scenes, each new scene revealing another segment of the future. In the first scene the Jews were chosen; in the second they received a constitution; in the third they acquired a homeland; in the fourth came the Prophets with a blueprint for mankind, and in the fifth the Torah was canonized. The nationalist team of Ezra and Nehemiah seems to be saying to the Jews, "Listen, Israel, do not disappear prematurely in the universality preached by the Prophets. You still have a mission to perform."

With Ezra and Nehemiah, the action shifted back to Jerusalem, where new adventures awaited the Jews.

9

From the Frying
Pan into the Fire

We now come to another incredible chapter in the amazing history of the Jews. The Persians, who had successfully preserved their empire for two centuries, were suddenly toppled from the summit by the new intellectual overlords of Europe—the Greeks. By the law of winner-take-all, the Jews passed from Persian to Greek rule.

Threatened by the bewitching lifestyle of the Greeks, the Jews, after a four-hundred year rest from fighting (500–142 B.C.E.), turned their plowshares into swords, and again went to war. They beat the hell out of the Greeks, and founded the second kingdom of Judah.

Who were these Greeks?

Starting out as barbaric tribes from northern India, the future Greeks plundered their way into Macedonia and down the Greek peninsula, casually exterminating the native populations. By 800 B.C.E., they reached Crete where they came in contact with its Semitic inhabitants. This encounter between barbaric Asiatic Indo-Europeans and cultured Semitic Cretans (known as Minoans) sparked a cultural revolution that was to eclipse the Semitic civilizations.

At about the time the Jews of the kingdom of Israel battled the Assyrians, the Greeks were founding the city-states of Athens, Sparta, and Corinth. In the two centuries between 500 and 300 B.C.E., Greece gave birth to a fantastic succession of leaders in practically every field of science and philosophy, art and literature, but not in religion, where she remained a backward, idolotrous nation.

The Greeks lived under the constant threat of their fellow Indo-Europeans, the Persians. Time after time the Greeks annihilated the invading Persians, but it did not occur to them to pursue the enemy to his homeland. As the Greeks saw it, why invade and be saddled with the task of governing, educating, and civilizing uncouth barbarians? Alexander the

Great of Macedonia, however, had a different idea. He would conquer and Hellenize the Persians, and thus create a Greek empire which he thought would endure forever and ever.

In 333 B.C.E., Alexander the Great, at age 23, crossed the Hellespont with thirty-two thousand infantry, and dealt the Persians a string of devastating defeats which took them out of history. Within a decade, Alexander's empire extended from Athens to India. At the age of 33 he was dead, and his empire died with him.

With the entry of the Jews into the orbit of Greek history, they were confronted with the greatest challenge since their enslavement in Egypt. The challenge in Egypt had been the loss of freedom. Now it was the exact opposite—total freedom. A head-on intellectual clash developed between Judaism and Hellenism. Which ideology would win in the free marketplace of ideas?

To Hellenize the people in his newly conquered empire, Alexander introduced a new method of indoctrination, not by the sword but by friendly relations. To facilitate the spread of Greek culture in occupied lands, Alexander commanded all his officers and men to intermarry and beget many children. So effective was this new method, that within ten years he founded twenty-five Greek cities in the Middle East. From them radiated the Greek language, the Greek way of life, Greek thought.

Though the Alexandrian empire lasted but twelve years, the influence of Hellenism itself persisted for six centuries. After Alexander's death (322 B.C.E.), his two top generals—Seleucus and Ptolomy—split the empire between them. Seleucus grabbed Asia Minor, founding the Seleucid empire, where the people became known as Syrians or as Seleucid Greeks or simply as Greeks. Ptolomy seized Egypt, founding the Ptolemaic dynasty which ruled Egypt for almost four hundred years.

Judah was first ruled by the Ptolomies, then was ceded to the Seleucids. As long as the Jews paid taxes and made no trouble, they had self-rule and religious freedom. In ever-greater numbers, the Jews turned from agriculture to business, commerce, and industry which took them to every corner of the Greek world. "They have penetrated into every state," wrote the Greek historian Strabo of the Jews, "so that it is difficult to find a single place in the world in which this tribe has not been received and become dominant."

Few pagans read the works of Greek philosophers or mused over Greek poetry, mainly because they were illiterate. But the literate Jews became mesmerized by Greek philosophy, science, and literature. They absorbed everything intellectual the Greeks had to offer. This encounter transformed them from biblical Jews to Hellenized Jews.

Greek life styles supplanted the old biblical way of life. The situation resembled that of the Jews in the United States after 1900, when the children of the Russian-Jewish immigrants gave up the ways of their

European ghetto-born parents for the American way of life. Under the impact of daily life, the educated Jews in the Grecian world began speaking Greek just as educated American Jews began speaking English. Greek names were adopted. Jews flocked to view the plays of the Greek dramatists; and to the horror of many a Jewish mother, male Jews took to wrestling in the nude in the gymnasia.

But underneath the tranquility smoldered resentment. A struggle was brewing between Judaism and Hellenism, creating a split in Jewish ranks. Two antagonistic religious-political parties developed, the Hellenizers and the anti-Hellenizers.

Just as Conservative, Reform, and many Orthodox Jews in America today accept much in the American way of life without feeling that they are compromising Judaism, so the Hellenizers in those days felt they could accept much in the Greek way of life without endangering their Judaism. And just as ultra-traditional Jews in America today want to keep things much as they had been in the ghettos of Europe in order to safeguard their brand of Judaism, so the anti-Hellenizing Jews believed that only by keeping things the way they had been before the Greeks showed up could they keep their concept of Judaism pure and alive.

Trouble began when the Seleucid rulers gave the political power to an extreme faction of the Hellenizers who introduced idol worship in the Jerusalem Temple. The anti-Hellenizers were in an uproar. Even the moderates thought things had gone too far when the new high priest, Jason, opened the Temple doors to pagan rites with Jewish priests officiating in Greek garb. Anger and hatred churned in the hearts of the anti-Hellenizers, who waited for a day of revenge. That chance came in 168 B.C.E.

A rumor had spread in Judah that the king, Antiochus Epiphanes, King of the Seleucid Empire, had been slain in a battle in Egypt. That did it. The anti-Hellenizers began a systematic slaughter of the radical Hellenizers by throwing them down the hundred-foot-high Temple wall. Few survived. After them went the Greek statues. Finished with the task of purifying the Temple, the anti-Hellenizers declared their independence from the rule of the Seleucids. (166 B.C.E.).

Alas, the rumor had been false. Antiochus was very much alive and full of wrath. He marched against Jerusalem, slaughtering the first ten thousand he encountered without inquiring into their religious affiliations. This senseless revenge united the moderates with the anti-Hellenizers against their new common enemy.

Had Antiochus stopped here, a grim, grinding twenty-four-year war might have been averted. His injured pride, however, did not permit this. Out of sheer anger, he acted upon some bad advice—that the only way to weaken the Jewish spirit was to destroy the Jewish religion. Antiochus outlawed the Sabbath, forbade circumcision, and decreed the Jews must eat pork. And, to top it all off, he installed a new gallery of idols in the

Temple. The ingredients were there for a second massive explosion. A minor incident sparked it.

In a small town outside Jerusalem, a Greek official tried to force a Jewish priest, Mattathias the Hasmonean, to sacrifice to Greek gods. Mattathias slew the official, whereupon he and his five sons headed for the hills. In great numbers, other Jews also rebelled. The resulting struggle became the first religious war in history.

Seething with indignation, Antiochus assembled a first-rate army. Confident of victory, he attached a battalion of slave auctioneers to it, and had posters placed throughout the realm quoting prices for Jewish slaves. But there was to be no slave auction. The Maccabees annihilated that army too, and in the year 164 B.C.E. recaptured Jerusalem. They purged the Temple for a second time of its new set of Greek statues and idols, and rededicated it to God.

The war between the Greeks and the Jews ground on for another twenty-one years. One by one Mattathias and four of his five sons were slain. Finally, the Seleucids called for an end to hostilities, and Simon, the only surviving son, signed the peace in 143 B.C.E. The impossible had been achieved: the kingdom of Judah had been restored. Simon was crowned the first king of the Hasmonean dynasty.

But the revolt which had been born in a blaze of religious glory, was destined to drown in political savagery. The subsequent eighty-year rule of the Hasmoneans became a macabre spree of fratricide, matricide, and regicide. The Hasmoneans killed each other and their enemies in casual abandon, as murder became a weapon of diplomacy.

Trouble started when some of the Hasmonean rulers tried to combine the throne of the king with the mantle of the high priest. The practice plunged the country into a series of fierce internal religious wars.

Luckily, the Hasmoneans had one good ruler, Queen Alexandra, who in spite of her brief nine-year rule (78–69 B.C.E.) ushered in an era called by some the "Golden Age." Following the advice of her brother, Rabbi Simon ben Shetach, she founded the world's first regular elementary schools and made education compulsory for all boys. Her brother also instituted the world's first teachers' college, in Jerusalem.

Upon Alexandra's death, yet another civil war broke out, resulting in the annexation of Judah by Rome. The civil war had been started by the two sons of Alexandra, each fighting for the vacant throne. Both brothers asked Rome for help. Rome obliged by sending her legions to Jerusalem, annexing the country, and renaming it Judea (63 B.C.E.).

If the Jews had thought anything would be better than another Hasmonean king, they guessed wrong. They got something worse—first a series of murderous Roman-appointed kings, and then a series of murderous Roman-appointed procurators.

The Jews had led a charmed life until now. They had survived four centuries of nomadic existence, four centuries of slavery in Egypt, two centuries of wars under Judges, five centuries of independence in two kingdoms, fifty years in Babylonian captivity, two centuries as a Persian satellite, a hundred-and-fifty years under Hellenistic rule, and a second bout of independence lasting eight decades. Could they survive the next challenge—a head-on collision with Rome? Very few people had.

10

The Glory That Was Judea and the Grandeur That Was Rome

Who were these Romans who treated the world as though it were their private property? Like the Greeks, the ancestors of the Romans also came from Asia. In the second millenium B.C.E., these pagans crossed the Alps and spread down the Italian peninsula. About the time Isaiah was preaching in Judah, legend has it that an animal, a wolf of unknown parentage, was nursing Romulus and Remus, the future founders of Rome (755 B.C.E.).

Three Punic Wars (284–146 B.C.E.) made the Romans masters of all Italy, Spain, and North Africa. Three Macedonian wars (215–148 B.C.E.) made them the masters of Greece and placed their legions on the periphery of Asia Minor. After annexing Egypt, Judah was next on their timetable of conquest.

The worst—and paradoxically the greatest—of the Roman appointed kings of Judea, was King Herod the Great (40 B.C.E.–4 C.E.)

Herod was an excellent administrator and diplomat. In spite of the Roman yoke, he stablized the country's economy, made Judea a power among Roman satellites, and rebuilt the Temple in Jerusalem which became an architectural wonder of its day.

But Herod was the archmurderer of his time. He murdered his rivals, his favorite wife Mariamne, several of his sons, and forty-five members of the Sanhedrin, the highest judicial body in the land. Though he was hated and despised by the Jews, he was tolerated by them because Mariamne, one of his ten wives, was a Hasmonean princess with whom he had two sons. The Jews hoped that eventually one of them would inherit the throne. But, in due course, Herod murdered them too.

Herod's successors were not much better. The Jews clamored for change and, to their surprise, the Romans listened to them. But it was a change for the worse. Instead of getting more murderous kings, they got the murderous procurators.

It is difficult to pick out the worst of the fourteen procurators who ruled Judea in the years 7 to 66 C.E. The most famous—or infamous—was Pontius Pilate, who condemned Jesus to death by crucifixion (30 or 34 C.E.).*

For the most part, these procurators were former crude soldiers who had worked their way up the ranks. All were bent on making an extra buck by extorting ever more taxes from the Jews, since they got a cut of the take. The proverbial last straw came in the year 66 with the last procurator, Florus, who demanded the equivalent of half a million dollars in protection money. The Jews lost patience. They flocked to the banners of the Zealots, a political party which advocated war against Rome. Under the leadership of the Zealots, the Jews stormed the Roman garrison outside Jerusalem, slaughtered the legionnaires, and sparked the Rome-Jerusalem war (66–70 C.E.)

Compared to this conflict, the much heralded battle of Marathon (400 B.C.E.) was a puny affair—eleven thousand Greeks against twenty-two thousand Persians. Alexander the Great needed but thirty-two thousand men to carve out his vast empire. Caesar had fewer than twenty-five thousand legionnaires with which to conquer Gaul (France and Germany) and Britain. But the Roman general Titus, in command of the Rome-Jerusalem war, had to use eighty thousand legionnaires and ten thousand cavalry to vanquish besieged Jerusalem. Jerusalem was defended by no more than twenty-three thousand Jewish soldiers. Yet it took the Romans four years to defeat the Jews.

During the first two years of the war, the Jews inflicted one humiliating defeat after another on the Roman armies. But in the end, Roman numbers won over Jewish valor. In the third year, the Romans at last stood outside the gates of Jerusalem. Certain that victory was within their grasp, Titus turned his ninety thousand men on the city. To his astonishment and horror, the Jews forced them back.

Realizing he could not win in a frontal assault, Titus decided to starve the city in a siege before attacking again. He sealed off Jerusalem with a fifteen-foot wall of dirt, and waited an entire year before daring another assault.

The end was inevitable. With battering rams and siege guns, the Romans tore gaps in the defenses; like termites they spilled into the city, taking gruesome revenge on the defenders for having made a mockery for four years of vaunted Roman valor. The Roman historian Tacitus records that some six-hundred thousand Jews were killed in the aftermath of that siege.

*Discussed in the next chapter.

Survivors of the carnage were paraded in a triumphal parade in Rome, sold as slaves, thrown off the Tarpeian Rock, or fed to the lions for amusement. "They (the Romans) made a desolation," observed a Roman historian, "and call it peace."

One of the greatest tourist attractions in Rome today is the triumphal Arch of Titus built to commemorate his victory over Judea. But it had been a devastating war for Rome, with frightening casualties. Few people question why a mighty emperor of a mighty empire should have bothered to commemorate such a costly victory over so small a nation as Judea. There are no triumphal arches in Rome to celebrate victories over the Carthaginians, the Greeks, the Egyptians, the French, the Germans, the British. But Titus was well aware that the crucial war had been the one with the Jews. The Arch of Titus still stands in Rome, but as a symbol of what? Of a vanished Roman Empire and the vanished Roman people? Or as a tribute to the indomitable spirit of the Jews, who did not vanish but still live as an unconquered people.

But the war was not over for the Romans. There was an aftermath to the fall of Jerusalem. The remnants of the Zealots—a total of 906 men, women, and children—under the leadership of Eleazar ben Yair, withdrew to Masada, twenty-five miles south of Jerusalem. This fortress had been built by Herod on a brown rock, steeply rising 1,200 feet toward the sky, its hem bordering on the Judean desert, overlooking the Dead Sea. Incredibly, this small remnant of Zealots withstood all Roman assaults for another two years.

Titus, now emperor, sent Flavius Silva, his best general, with four thousand legionnaires to take this rock and put an end to Jewish resistance. Repulsed time and again, Silva resorted to using Jewish slave-labor battalions to build a ramp of earth from the desert floor to the top of the fortress. After several unsuccessful efforts and staggering casualties, he finally stormed it.

What happened to the defenders? There is still a great debate among scholars. Some contend that the defenders fought to the last individual; others maintain that they committed mass suicide. Probably a combination of the two took place. Reduced in numbers after two years of fighting, the Zealots realized all hope was lost. The surviving defenders probably killed the women and children as an alternative to having them raped and sold as slaves by the victorious Romans, then fought on to the last man. Not a single defender was taken alive. Even the hardened Roman soldiers were impressed with this bravery.

The defeat at Masada should have marked the end of the Jewish people. But it did not. The spirit of Eleazar ben Yair was not dead; it was to erupt in two more revolts.

The next revolt flared up in 113 c.e., not in Judea but outside of it. It was the world's first Diaspora revolt—by Jews living in Egypt, Crete, Cyprus, Cyrene. Though spontaneous, unorganized, leaderless, and doomed to defeat, its ferocity stunned the Romans, who finally quelled the uprising after two years.

Two revolts had taught the Romans not to underestimate the Jews, but they were not prepared for yet a third uprising which broke out in 132 C.E. It, too, had no counterpart in history, since it was led by a unique team—a self-proclaimed messiah on horseback, Simon bar Kochba, and his apostle, the renowned Rabbi Akiba.

Bar Kochba was an irascible messiah whose devotion to God was tinged with a little skepticism. He is said to have once exclaimed before a battle, "Lord, you don't have to help us, but don't spoil it for us either." Rabbi Akiba, the greatest and most revered Jewish scholar of his time, confirmed Bar Kochba's messiahship, thus saving Bar Kochba from excommunication by the Sanhedrin which did not take too kindly to his claim.

In desperation, the Romans again had to recall one of their ablest generals, Julius Septimus Severus, from Britain where he was engaged in another war. Severus arrived in Judea at the head of a crack force. If Severus had looked for an easy victory, he was to be disappointed.

Severus, unable to win in open warfare, resorted to total warfare, killing everything that moved, burning anything that did not, leaving total devastation in his wake. The merciless butchery continued for three years until the final battle at Bethar, in 135 C.E., where Bar Kochba was killed and Rabbi Akiba captured and tortured to death.

To the Romans, the Jews were troublemakers. Instead of thanking the Romans for having conquered them and making them Roman citizens, the Jews had rebelled three times, setting a bad example for docile satellites. It was time for the Romans to teach the Jews the "Carthaginian lesson."

In the third century B.C.E., the Carthaginians had established a small empire in North Africa. In the three Punic Wars, the Carthaginians, like the Jews, had challenged Rome's rule. By 146 B.C.E., the Romans had had enough. "Delenda est Carthago!"—"Carthage must be destroyed!"— thundered consul Marcus Cato in the Roman senate. And in the third Punic War, Carthage was levelled to the ground, much of the population killed and enslaved, and the remnant exiled. It spelled an end to the Carthaginians who, like the Jews from the kingdom of Israel, could not survive defeat and disappeared.

Now the Jews of Judea were given the Carthaginian treatment. They were banned from Jerusalem; the city was renamed Aelia Capitolina, and a temple to Zeus was built where Herod's Temple had stood. Very few Jews remained in the land. Most of the population not already slain was sold into slavery or expelled into the vastness of the Roman empire, the new total Diaspora. For the next two thousand years, the Jews would not have a country of their own.

Even though some historians attribute anti-Semitism to the Romans for this treatment of the Jews, the Jews did not think of themselves as victims of anti-Semitism. In fact, no such word existed in the vocabulary of Jews, Greeks, or Romans. The Jews knew that an army neither gave nor asked for mercy. Killing Jews was no different from killing any other rebellious people. The Jews knew they would be decimated if they lost because they were the enemy, just as they would decimate their enemies. It was not until a thousand years later that anti-Semitism was to appear and under totally different circumstances with totally different aims.

Would the Jews of Judah now disappear? After all, they had already hung on for two thousand years. Would this total dispersion obliterate them?

Will there be a new rescue team, another Moses with a new code of law, another King David with a conquering sword? Or would there be a new string of prophets to write new guidelines for survival, another messiah armed to rally the dispirited Jews into a new Zionade?

It was to be none of these. Jewish history is too inventive.

But before taking up the thread of future adventures of the Jewish people in the second act of their history, we must retrace our steps back to the days of the Roman procurator Pontius Pilate—back to the days when a Jew named Jesus walked the streets of Jerusalem in 30 C.E., because the life and death of Jesus had a great impact on the course of future Jewish history in Christian Europe.

11
Jews, Jesus, and Pilate

Who is Jesus whom almost one billion Christians consider divine, and to whom serfs, priests, and nobles have knelt in homage for nineteen centuries? Who is this Jesus, in whose name people were burned alive in the flames of *autos-da-fé*, in whose name Crusades were launched to convert by force people of other faiths, yet in whose spirit was created Western civilization, the most magnificent civilization in the history of man?

History has a simple answer. Jesus was a Jew, born of Jewish parents in a kosher home, and circumcized on the eighth day. He was born sometime between 4 B.C.E. and 4 C.E.* in the town of Nazareth in the province of Galilee in Judea, then under Roman rule. Thirty years later the Roman procurator Pontius Pilate sentenced him to death by crucifixion on the charge of sedition against Rome. Not until twenty years after his death did he become known as a Christian.

This is all history knows about the man Jesus. All else is theology based on the New Testament, of which the four Gospels form its heart. Since Jesus himself never wrote anything, we know of his life mainly through these four Gospels.

The earliest Gospel (though second in the New Testament) was written by Mark after 70 C.E., followed by the Gospel of Matthew and Luke, written around 85 and 90 C.E. respectively. The last, by John, was composed sometime after the year 110 C.E. Thus the first Gospel was not written until forty years after the death of Jesus, and the last as late as eighty years after.

Many scholars question the Gospel accounts of the life and ministry of Jesus because all four accounts contain statements which cannot be

---

*For chronological convenience, history has now accepted the date of the birth of Jesus as 1 C.E.

proved by history. Also, what Mark says is often contradicted by Matthew and Luke, who often contradict each other. All three are frequently contradicted by John. The testimony of one evangelist often invalidates the testimony of another.

The historic career of Jesus begins around 30 C.E., when, at the age of thirty, he is baptized by John the Baptist. This symbolic anointment by water explains the name "Jesus Christ." "Jesus" is the Greek equivalent for the Jewish name of Joshua. "Christ" is the Greek word meaning "to anoint." Thus "Jesus Christ" simply means "Joshua the anointed."

After his baptism, Jesus took up the life of a preacher. There was nothing un-Jewish in his early teachings from that of the Judaism of his times. He observed the Mosaic law and, in the tradition of the Prophets, taught compassion for the poor, mercy, and tolerance. His Sermon on the Mount, for instance, consists of paraphrased sentences from the Old Testament, as do his famed sayings known as the Beatitudes.

As he wandered through Galilee, Jesus gathered twelve disciples. One day, he unveiled his future destiny to them, which placed him on a collision course with the Romans. According to the Gospels, Jesus predicted to his disciples that he would be arrested upon reaching Jerusalem, that he would be tried and condemned to death on the cross by the Romans, and that he would then rise (that is, be resurrected) after three days. Then, after having outlined his future, Jesus went toward Jerusalem to seek its fulfillment.

That year Jerusalem was a proverbial powder keg. Rebellion after rebellion was sweeping the troubled land of Judea as freedom fighters staged one uprising after another against Rome. Among these freedom fighters was a group of Zealots known as Sicarii, whose specialty was killing Romans with special daggers called sicarii, hence their name.

When Jesus entered Jerusalem, a week before Passover, excitement was running high. A new rebellion had recently been quelled in Galilee by the Romans, and there was talk of another revolt. The new Roman procurator, Pontius Pilate, had left his palace at Caesaria, at the head of a legion, to take personal command.

What now happens is obscured by conflicting testimony in the Gospels, much of it not supported by history.

In essence, the Gospels state that those Jews who did not believe that Jesus was the messiah conspired to have him arrested. He was taken to the Sanhedrin for a night trial presided over by the high priest. This high priest, say the evangelists, sent men out into the night to search for fake witnesses to testify against him. According to the Gospels, Jesus was convicted by the Sanhedrin on perjured testimony; then, the next morning, dragged by the Jews to Pontius Pilate for a second trial, with the demand that he crucify Jesus for them.

Scholars find it difficult to accept these Gospel accounts as historic facts. According to Jewish law, they point out, no one could be arrested at night. To hold court proceedings after sundown was illegal. The great Sanhedrin could not convene in the palace of the high priest and it could not initiate an arrest or sentence anyone to death, unless two witnesses had first sworn out charges against the accused. Such action by the Sanhedrin was as unlikely as the Supreme Court justices of the United States ordering a citizen seized at night, then hunting for an informer to testify falsely against the accused, convicting him to death without a trial, and having him executed first thing the next morning. The Sanhedrin, like the United States Supreme Court, simply never operated that way.

Some historians today believe that Jesus was one of many Jewish rebels against Roman rule, and that his disciples were mostly Galilean Zealots. Could it be, speculate these historians, that Jesus entered Jerusalem as a self-proclaimed messiah, was arrested by the Jews to prevent his capture by the hated Romans, and held in protective custody until Pilate would depart Jerusalem, and the danger to Jesus was over?

But Pilate, suspecting Jesus of being a Zealot, demanded that the Jews hand Jesus over to him. This would explain why all four Gospel accounts state that Jesus was taken from the Jews, delivered to Pilate for a trial, and sentenced to death by him for the crime of sedition—for aspiring to become king of the Jews.

All historic evidence points to a Roman atrocity, not to a case of Jewish injustice. The Gospels themselves tell us that at the scene of the crucifixion it is the Jews who mourn the death of Jesus whereas the Roman soldiers played dice for his mantle and mocked him as the king of the Jews with a crown of thorns.

For the first twenty years after the death of Jesus, most people known as Christians were Jews, and Christianity was one Jewish sect among twenty-four different sects in the Jerusalem of that time. The great schism between the Nazarenes (as the Christians were known then) and the Jews did not take place until Saul of Tarsus, now better known by his Roman name Paul, converted to Christianity and broke with the Jewish tradition (52 C.E.). Paul preached the new faith to the pagans who soon outnumbered the Jewish members. One by one Paul abandoned the dietary law, circumcision, and the rest of the laws of Moses until Christianity was no longer a Jewish sect. By the end of the first century C.E., the Romans looked upon the Christians, not as a sect of Judaism, but as a distinct, new religion.

The reasons why Christians consider Jesus divine need not concern us here. Suffice it to say that the Christian idea has been rejected not only by the Jews but also by seventy-five percent of the world's population—by three billion out of four billion people. Also, through defections in Russia and Eastern Europe, Christianity has lost over three-hundred million adherents since World War I.

In the fourth century, however, the Christians, though still a minority religion in the Roman empire, gained political power. The Jews were then confronted with a new danger to their existence, as the Christians made it their special mission to convert the Jews to Christianity. In a subsequent chapter we shall discuss this aspect. Meanwhile, let us return to the Jews waiting in the lobby of history for their cue to plunge headlong into the first challenge of the second act.

For an understanding of what is about to happen, we must go back in time to 70 C.E. and the first revolt of the Jews against the Romans, back to besieged Jerusalem where a momentous debate took place which literally shaped the subsequent two thousand years of Jewish destiny.

THE SECOND ACT

The Second 2,000 Years—
From ben Zakkai to Ben-Gurion
(100 B.C.E.–2000 C.E.)

*"From Zion shall go forth the Law, and the word of
God from Jerusalem," prophesied Isaiah. Like King
David carrying the Ark into battle, so the victorious
Jews, in their reconquest of Israel two millenia later,
carried the Torah with them—reaffirming the words
of Isaiah.*

דברי הרב ודברי התלמיד דברי מי שומעין

דרבא אמרי אפילו מיום ראשון ואילך: השונא כל שלא דבר כו׳
מנלן קרי ביה והוא לא אויב לו ולא אוהב הוא אלא סברא הוא דלא אויב ולא מבקש רעתו
מאי טעמא משום דמרחקא דעתיה אהב נמי מקרבא דעתיה והאי אויב הוא ולא אוהב הוא ולא מבקש
רעתו לו מאי לא אויב לו ולא אוהב הוא ולא מבקש רעתו לו מבקש רעתו הוא איבה בדין כדאמרה **מתני** את כל האדם לחובה היו מבקשין
לו מזכה וחובה ומזכין מחייבין הדיינים גמרו את הדבר היו מכניסין אותן הגדול שבדיינים אומר איש פלוני אתה זכאי איש פלוני אתה חייב ומניין לכשיצא לא יאמר אני מזכה וחביריי מחייבין אבל מה אעשה שהיו רבי עלי על זה נאמר (ויקרא יט) לא תלך רכיל בעמך ואומר הולך רכיל מגלה סוד

גמ היכי אמרי להו
בממתא שקר אמר (ליה) רבא יכול למימר שב שני הוה כפנא ואבבא אומנא
לא חליף אמר (ליה) רב אשי אמר ליה אמרינן להו ממפ* ודרב וחזן שנן שב שני הוה מותנא ואינש בלא שניה לא שכיב מכלל דבעי רחמי ויהיבו ליה
אמרינן להו סהדי שקרי אאוגרתכון זילי דכתיב ויהושיבו שנים אנשים בני
בליעל נגדו ויעידהו לאמר ברכת אלהים ומלך: אם אמר הוא אמר לי כך מאי איכא
למימר דא"ר יהודה אמר רב כנה לי בידך אמר לו הן למד לי מנה ד׳ בידך אמר לו הן
משמה אני בך פטור (תניא נמי הכי מנה לי בידך אמר לו הן למד לו הן למד
לו תנהו לי בך פטור אלא עד שיאמרו עדים אתה חייבו לו מנה ד׳ בידך אמר לו הן תנהו לי
בך פטור אלא עד שיאמר לו מנה לי בידך אמר לו הן למד לו תנהו לי
פלוני ופלוני אמר לו כתירא אני בך שמא תטפוני לדין למחר מסת מנה אמר לו עדים
חסרו מיהודה והכי איכא קני

רבינו חננאל

(בסוף הסוגיא)

PART I

Adventures among the Romans, Sassanids, and Arabs

(100 B.C.E.–1200 C.E.)

The Jews augment the Torah with Mishna to meet the competition for mens' minds in the Greco-Roman world; enrich the Mishna with Gemara to survive the Sassanid challenge; and combine Mishna and Gemara into the Talmud as a response to the lure of the Muslim civilization.

The Talmud—the Oral Law designed for survival in the Diaspora. It kept the Jews within the orbit of their faith as history hurled them through six civilizations in the time span from ben Zakkai to Ben Gurion.

12
The Great Debate

There is a prayer in Jewish liturgy said only on the High Holy Days which begins: "On Rosh Hashanah it is inscribed, on Yom Kippur the decree is sealed . . . who shall die and who shall live."

The Rome-Jerusalem war (66–70 C.E.) is such a decree in Jewish history. A great debate swept Jerusalem during those four years, with the life and death of the Jewish people hanging on the choice they would make.

Jerusalem was torn between two political parties, which, though they had no names, could be labeled the "war party" and the "peace party." The War Party, led by Eleazer ben Yair, the heroic defender of Masada, stood for a military showdown with Rome. The Peace Party, whose most prominent member was Johanan ben Zakkai, stood for military surrender to Rome.

In essence this was the stand of the war party: "Our salvation lies in a war with Rome now. Joshua did not win the battle of Jericho by leading peace brigades chanting surrender. King David did not forge the Jewish kingdom playing his harp and singing psalms. We Jews persevered by standing on our feet, fighting for our freedom. Shall we now fall to our knees and beg for mercy? No! Let us take to our swords as we did under the Maccabees to make Jewish life safe for future generations."

And this, in essence, was the stand of the peace party: "We concur with everything our brave opponents say, except their conclusion. They are men of valor, but of little vision. They speak of the past; we speak of the future. Though Rome wants political submission, she holds no hostility toward our religion. Let us avoid annihilation in battle and surrender; when the right time comes, we can again strike for political freedom. Meanwhile, let us prepare ourselves spiritually for the coming exile, and thus guarantee the survival of Judaism, for without Judaism there can be no Jews."

The war party won the debate. The death penalty was decreed for anyone advocating surrender.

We know the fate that befell Jerusalem and the fate of Eleazer ben Yair. But what happened to Johanan ben Zakkai?

Johanan ben Zakkai, an aged scholar, was the greatest rabbi of his generation, renowned for his learning and humanism. Trapped in doomed Jerusalem, ben Zakkai could foresee the final disaster. He knew the measures the Romans would take to quell this uprising. He also knew that no matter how heroically the Jews would fight, it would spell the decimation of his people and the end of Judaism if his counsel for peace did not prevail.

Ben Zakkai had a plan to save Judaism. To do it, he had to get to the ear of the Roman General, Vespasian, then besieging the city. But how? Trying to escape from the city meant instant death at the hands of the Zealots if caught.

To get into besieged Troy, the Greeks had resorted to the ruse of a Trojan horse to get out of besieged Jerusalem, ben Zakkai resorted to the ruse of a coffin.* Ben Zakkai got inside. His disciples carried his "body" into the streets, loudly lamenting that their beloved teacher had died of cholera. Fearing an outbreak of this dreaded plague, the Zealots allowed the disciples to bury ben Zakkai outside the city gates. But once outside, they carried him instead to the Roman lines.

Regretably, history does not record what General Vespasian thought of this patrician patriarch who had arrived in a coffin, alive. What did ben Zakkai want from him? Certainly not to spare his life, for he had risked it by coming to see him.

To Vespasian's amazement, the patriarchal Jew predicted that he, General Vespasian, would soon be made emperor of the Roman empire. And should this happen, the patriarch asked, would General Vespasian grant him permission to found an academy for the study of Jewish Scripture in the town of Jabneh?

Stunned by the prophecy, and surprised by the modesty of the request, Vespasian agreed, provided the prophecy came true. What possible harm could come out of granting an old fool the right to study the superstitions surrounding the worship of an invisible God?

Within a year, Vespasian did become emperor. Ben Zakkai had based his prediction not on black magic but on a shrewd guess. The latest emperor, Nero, had died a whimpering death when a slave, at his request, had thrust a dagger in his throat. Sooner of later, ben Zakkai surmised, the strongest man in the empire would emerge as the emperor. Time proved him correct; within a few months, Vespasian was offered the throne. Before leaving for Rome to become emperor, Vespasian entrusted the conclusion of the war to his son Titus. Vespasian also kept his promise to ben Zakkai.

Was ben Zakkai a hero or a traitor for deserting his fellow Jews by

*Other scholars say it was a shroud.

leaving besieged Jerusalem? Did his purpose excuse his means? History tells us he won immediate fame as a hero.

History does not tell us why another famous Jew, a contemporary of ben Zakkai, went down in Jewish history as a traitor though he seemingly committed the same act of surrender as ben Zakkai had. He is Flavius Josephus (known also by the Jewish name, Joseph ben Matthias), famed historian who wrote the only eyewitness account of the war with Rome in his classic *History of the Jewish War.*

Josephus was the general in command of the Jewish forces for the first two years of the war with Rome. As it progressed, Josephus, like ben Zakkai, became convinced that the Jews could not win, but were only inviting disaster. As he could not convince the Zealot leaders of his cause, he capitulated to the Romans. For this the Jews promptly branded him a traitor.

The Roman emperor granted Josephus permission to accompany the Roman army to write an account of the war. It is the only known work which speaks of the bravery of the Jews in that war. Though the book often portrays the Jews in a more favorable light than the Romans, it was not censored. And let it be said in defense of Josephus that, though now and then he defers to the Romans, he neither licks their sandals nor does he ever derogate the Jews.

Masada and Jabneh have each come to stand for a symbol in Jewish history—Masada for resistance and Jabneh for surrender. Today, Israeli paratroopers, upon graduating from their training, are brought to Masada where they take an oath never to surrender. Jabneh, however, is not glorified.

Which is the true spirit of the Jews? Masada or Jabneh? The answer is both. Each was the right response for its own time. Just as Joshua made the right choice by taking to the sword in the conquest of Canaan to get Jewish history on the road, so ben Zakkai made the equally right choice by choosing surrender to insure the future of Jewish destiny.

The lesson of Masada is as unmistakable as the lesson of Jabneh. At Masada we saw Judaism die symbolically with the death of every defender. At Jabneh we saw the Jews survive and with them Judaism. The Zealots who died at Masada had looked to the past; the Jews who opted for Jabneh had looked to the future. The secret of Jewish survival lies in making the right choice at the right time!

(In our own days, we come across this same debate. The Zionists in the nineteenth century had correctly appraised a new disease of the modern age, anti-Semitism, which threatened the existence of the Jews. They knew no accommodation could be made with the forces of anti-Semitism, which demanded the death of Jews for no other reason than that of being Jews. The word, not accommodation, was the correct response, and history rewarded the Jews for that choice with the independent state of Israel.)

The emperor kept his word, and the followers of ben Zakkai traded political surrender for religious freedom. But with that surrender came a great divide in Jewish history. The Jew who, from the time of the Exodus from Egypt until his surrender to Rome, had been an *ish milhama*, a man of war, now became a man of peace who would try to solve his problems not with the sword but with reason and prayer.

The first two thousand years of Jewish history from Abraham to ben Zakkai, is our first act. The next two thousand years—from ben Zakkai, the man of peace, to Ben-Gurion, the man of war—will be our second act.

In this second act of their odyssey through history, the Jews will encounter six challenges as history tosses them from civilization to civilization—each civilization constituting a separate challenge. We shall see the Jews tossed successively from the hedonistic Greco-Roman world into the tolerant atmosphere of the Sassanid empire, into the open society of the Islamic civilization, into the closed society of the feudal world, into the regression of the ghetto, into the sick society of the modern scientific age—to be finally hurled, at the end of the Second Act, back to the vortex of their history, back to Israel where they had started two thousand years before.

In these two thousand years of Diaspora life, full of the most incredible adventures, Jewish history came up with some of the most implausible but effective survival ideas.

13
Rabbis to the Rescue

Who were the rabbis?

The Torah does not mention them; it only speaks of priests. When, then, did the rabbis enter Jewish history?

The rabbis were the answer to the challenge of the destruction of the Temple in the Rome-Jerusalem war. They entered Jewish history unobtrusively toward the end of the First Act (100 B.C.E.) and were firmly in power at the start of the Second Act (100 C.E.). Their function was to take the place of the priests who were becoming anachronistic figures in a fast changing Roman world.

We saw how, during the years of the Babylonian captivity, the intrepid Jews had developed synagogue Judaism to take the place of priestly Judaism. But we also saw how, with the return to Jerusalem during the first Zionade, the Jews rebuilt the Temple and anointed Jeshua as high priest. Priestly Judaism was back in power.

But it was not the end of synagogue Judaism. Other Jews, trickling back to Jerusalem after the Zionades, preferred their Babylonian synagogue Judaism to the revived priestly Judaism. They began building synagogues in Jerusalem as early as the third century B.C.E. As the number of synagogues increased, so did the influence of these synagogue Jews.

As one might expect, friction developed between synagogue Jews and Temple Jews. Soon two political parties emerged—one, the Sadducees, representing the Temple society of priests and aristocrats; the other, the Pharisees, representing the synagogue society of sages and the common people. By the dawn of the first century C.E., there were about a hundred synagogues in Jerusalem. In the coming struggle for power, the Pharisees won. The final showdown came after the Rome-Jerusalem war.

The priests sat around—symbolically—wringing their hands, bemoaning their sad state, jobless in the wake of the Roman destruction of the Temple. Judaism was dead, they lamented.

Not at all, rejoined the sages, the teachers of the new synagogue Judaism. Judaism was alive and doing well, they claimed. Why not come to the synagogues dedicated to the ideals of the Prophets. No expensive heifers needed for sacrifice—only prayer and a willing heart.

What the sages said made sense to many Jews. But still many doubted. "How can we stay Jewish?" they wondered. "We are dispersed in many lands. Look at the problems we have. Does the Torah have the answers?"

"Yes," said the sages. "The answer to all problems are in the Torah. It is merely a matter of searching Scripture for the right answer."

And so the sages changed themselves into interpreters of the Torah. Their interpretations became known as Mishna, the oral law, in contrast to the Torah itself, which was the written law. The teachers of the Mishna became known as the Tannaim, the Repeaters, or one could say the interpreters of the law.

Actually, the process of the Mishna had begun several centuries before the destruction of the Temple. In its early days, the growth of the Mishna had been governed by few rules. But as the Mishna grew in popularity, Pharisee leaders wanted a more scientific basis for the Mishna to give their interpretations greater validity. The man who achieved this goal was Hillel, born toward the end of the first century B.C.E.

There are two versions of the life of Hillel. One shows him as a poor youth who drifted from Babylonia to Jerusalem in search of a higher education. In true Horatio Alger fashion, he graduated at the top of his class, rising from the rags of a pauper to the mantle of the president of the Sanhedrin, the highest judicial body in the land.

The other version holds that Hillel was born in Alexandria, which would account for the fact that he spoke fluent Greek. This view contends that Hillel was a rich man's son who was forty years old when he came to Jerusalem where his vast learning earned him instant respect.

Hillel's greatest contribution to Judaism was in structuring a scientific foundation for the Mishna. He was the author of the seven middot, seven rules of logic, which he used to discover new meanings in the Torah in the same way that scientists today use logic to discover new laws of nature. In essence, the Mishna had the same relationship to the Torah as American constitutional law has to the Constitution. In the same way that Mishna interpretations were derived by inference from the Torah, so constitutional law is derived by inference from the Constitution.

It was in the generation after Hillel that the title Rabbi, literally meaning "my master," was conferred on the sages.

This method of extracting new meanings out of the Torah was not accepted by the Sadducees who were strict constructionists. They sided with the priests in denouncing Mishna Judaism as false Judaism. They could not see how there could be a Judaism without priests and sacrifice. But the tide of history was against them. With the destruction of the Temple by the Romans and the expulsion of the Jews from Jerusalem, the Sadducee version of Judaism withered. As Mishna Judaism grew in popularity, the rabbis began displacing the priests.

Ben Zakkai had correctly guessed that the Mishna as an oral law was the new wave of Judaism. Soon after the fall of Jerusalem, he opened his academy of oral law in Jabneh, a former Philistine city northwest of Jerusalem.

Ben Zakkai's greatness was not in originating new Mishna, but in making the new oral law a portable tabernacle that could be carried in one's mind and heart, and made to flourish in any land.

But how could the message of the Mishna reach the Jews, scattered as they were throughout the four corners of the world? Who would be its messengers, and how could it be carried into the vastness of the Roman empire?

Jewish history is too capricious for anyone to make an educated guess. Not even Alexandre Dumas could have come up with a more colorful cast of rescuers—not three musketeers armed with rapiers but three intellectuals armed with quills. They were Gamaliel II, a businesman turned scholar who sold ben Zakkai's ideas to the Diaspora Jews; Akiba, a rabbi turned warrior, who strengthened the Mishna with social legislation; and Judah Hanasi, a prince of the house of David, who codified the Mishna.

14

The Call of the Mishna

When ben Zakkai died in 80 C.E., his successor, Gamaliel II, a wealthy aristocrat who consorted with Roman emperors and lived like a prince on his vast estates, brought about an amazing change in Jewish fortunes. He proposed that Rome should establish a patriarchate of rabbis to rule the remaining Jews in Palestine, with himself as the first ruler. Quick to acknowledge past mistakes, the Romans recognized the rabbinate as the new voice of the Jews and conferred the title Nasi, prince, on Gamaliel and his successors.

Gamaliel appointed himself salesmanager for the new rabbinic Judaism and travelled throughout the Diaspora to spread the new idea of a universal halacha or Jewish law, binding on all Jews wherever they were. He was especially concerned with the inroads the Christians were making in Jewish ranks. The Christian apostle Paul had initiated the practice of preaching Christian doctrine from pulpits in Jewish synagogues, and other Christian missionaries continued the practice. The Jews listened to these strange doctrines, some wondering where in the Torah God had said what the Christians proclaimed, others thinking it was merely another variety of Judaism. Herein lay the danger.

Gamaliel ended this practice of a free ride for Christian doctrine in Jewish synagogues by inserting a sentence of excommunication into the Jewish liturgy: "May the slanderers be destroyed and removed from the book of life." That did it. The Christians became angry and withdrew their membership from Jewish congregations. They built meeting halls of their own, modelled on the synagogue, which became known as churches, thus making the Jews the midwife assisting in the birth of the church.

But Gamaliel was also the spokesman for the new oral law. So effective was his preaching and pounding that, wherever he visited, Christianity made few or no inroads among Jewish ranks. The Christians therefore turned their proselytizing efforts away from the Jews to concentrate on the pagans. Here they succeeded. Christianity, which began as a Jewish sect, became a religion of former pagans in the Roman empire.

The next of the triumvirate was Rabbi Akiba (40–135 C.E.) who had certified the messiahship of Bar Kochba. Akiba realized that man does not live by ethics alone but also by bread and butter. The wars with Rome had created large numbers of landless farmers and unemployed workers. Under his influence, the Mishna began to reflect social changes. Labor, for instance, was protected, and the rights of women enlarged. Though he also tried to ban superstition, he failed. The people loved it.

The stage is now set for Judah Hanasi (about 135–220 C.E.), a descendant of the royal house of David, who consorted with Roman aristocracy and counted Emperor Marcus Aurelius among his friends. He was a great admirer of Roman law and the way it was organizaed into a cohesive code. Impressed by its organization, Hanasi undertook to codify and bring order to the three-century growth of the Mishna, systematizing and arranging the material according to subject matter.

With the hauteur born of superior intellect and scholarship, Hanasi omitted whatever he deemed irrelevant, even though he did include the most varied material from a broad range of scholars preceding him. Because of the reverence the people held for him, few dared to challenge his decisions.

Judah Hanasi's code gained total acceptance by the people within his lifetime. Even to this day, his edition and codification is considered the Mishna. He not only codified it, but in effect also closed it. He declared that, just as with the Torah, nothing new could be added to the Mishna either.

Though Judah Hanasi gave no reason for his action, some scholars surmise it was because he feared that, if not curbed, the Mishna might some day rival the Torah in authority.

In retrospect, we can see how these three rabbis had boldly taken over the Mishna as a vehicle for survival in the Diaspora. But the Mishna was essentially a religious work, governing the new precepts of Judaism and how to stay Jewish in a diaspora. However, answers to non-religious problems were not always found in the Mishna. In the first six centuries after the Rome-Jerusalem war, Jewish leaders forged a remarkable series of diaspora survival laws, many valid to this very day.

What were some of the salient dangers threatening Jewish solidarity and what measures did Jewish leaders advocate to avert them?

To avert the danger of Jews disappearing though slavery, these leaders affirmed the biblical injunction that every Jew was his brother's keeper. Thus they decreed that any Jew sold into slavery had to be ransomed by the nearest Jewish community within seven years.

To prevent the Jewish religion from being fragmentized, Jewish liturgy and prayers were standardized.

To ensure that Jewish communities would not disappear, it was decreed that wherever ten males over the age of thirteen lived within walking distance they had to establish a religious community, the minyan. As soon as there were 120 males over the age of thirteen, they had to establish a Jewish social community, including a court of their own to adjudicate according to Jewish law.

Each community had to raise taxes to support itself, the principle upon which present-day organizations, such as the Jewish Federation and the United Fund, rest. The Jews had to be self-supporting, never appeal to the host community for charity, and never be a burden to the host state.

It was against Jewish law for a Jew to go hungry; charity had to be provided with dignity to those who needed it. Each Jewish Diaspora community was reponsible for its own school system; education had to be provided free to the needy and to orphans.

With these and similar enactments, the Jews in Diaspora settlements developed into proud, independent communities which respected learning, rejected laziness, fostered responsibility, and practiced thrift and charity. They dignified the work of freemen above that of slaves, put the freedom of every man above privileged rights of noblemen, and elevated their moral concepts above the daily bestiality of the pagans. More of these Diaspora survival laws were to be passed as fate sent the Jews from one civilization to another in this Second Act.

By the fifth century, the main threat to the Jews had been averted. But new dangers loomed on the horizon. The Roman empire had begun its long slide into oblivion. She was beset with the external problem of barbarian invasions and the internal problem of subversion by the Christians. Palestine became the corridor for invading armies. Those forced to stay were raped, enslaved, or killed if caught in the path of the invaders. The rich, in the main, fled to Rome. The intellectuals, in the main, fled first to the Parthian, then to the Sassanid empires.

The exodus of the Jews from Palestine increased after each rebellion against Rome. By the time of the death of Judah Hanasi, the center of Jewish life had shifted from the Greco-Roman world to the Parthian empire.

What will happen to the Jews? What will the United Jewish Diaspora Rescue Team come up with now?

15

Here Comes the Gemara

Who were the Parthians?

To this very day many Jewish scholars persist in calling the Parthian empire "Babylonia." In a curious sort of way they are correct. The Parthian empire was formerly the Seleucid empire, formerly the Persian empire, and formerly the Babylonia empire.

The breakup of the Seleucid empire began shortly after its war with the Maccabees, when a nomadic people known as the Parthians, swooped down on it from the steppes of Turkestan. In a series of wars lasting over several decades, the Parthians dismembered the Seleucid empire and imposed their rule on the ruins.

The Jews adjusted themselves to the situation and changed their citizenship from Seleucid to Parthian. Before they settled down to the serious business of succeeding as Parthian Jews, a comic-opera interlude occurred.

Two Jewish brothers, Asineus and Anileus, decided to go into the empire business for themselves. Having been former cattle rustlers, they organized a band of outlaws and wrested a sizable chunk of land from the Parthians, converting it into a private kingdom. But it did not last long. One brother was poisoned and the other killed in battle, ending the Jewish-Parthian kingdom.

But there was a happy result. The Parthians decided to forgive and forget this little act of treason because the Jews were excellent soldiers who hated the Romans as much as the Parthians did. The Parthians granted the Jews self-rule under a Jewish prince of the house of David, who became known as the Resh Galuta, Hebrew for head of the exile, or by its Greek term, exilarch.

The Exilarch had royal powers. He appointed Jewish judges, was supported by Jewish taxes, and lived on a large estate staffed by slaves. History had handed the Jews new freedoms on a royal platter.

Jews fleeing the Roman empire in the wake of their wars with Rome, made Parthia their first choice, much as two thousand years later Russian Jews fleeing Communist Russia made the United States their first choice.

After a three-hundred-year rule (roughly between 100 B.C.E. and 200 C.E.), the Parthian paradise for the Jews came to an end as history substituted one paradise for another. The new one was the Sassanid empire.

Who, then, were the Sassanids? They were the remains of the Persian empire after its defeat by Alexander the Great, and the ancestors of the Iranians today.

In 226 C.E., the grandson of a priest named Sasan (hence the name Sassanid), whose ancestors were Persians, led an army against the Parthians, defeated them, and converted the former Parthians into loyal Sassanids.

And what happened to the Jews? They became loyal Sassanid Jews. The Sassanids continued the lenient policies of the Parthians, the only difference being that now the Exilarch was a Sassanid Jew instead of a Parthian Jew, though still of the house of David.

The Sassanids ushered in an age of splendor and prosperity in which the Jews fully participated. Jewish women began to enjoy unheard of freedoms. Though polygamy for males was not as yet forbidden, it began to disappear. Women now had so many rights and privileges that it became too costly for a man to maintain more than one wife.

Up until the beginning of the third century C.E., the Jews in the Sassanid empire had been intellectual underachievers. But as more scholars fled Palestine, they sparked a Jewish cultural reawakening.

Judah Hanasi had tried to stem this brain drain from Palestine by refusing to ordain rabbis who wanted to leave the country. But he failed. Hanasi's students defied him and took the Mishna with them. But the Mishna, which concerned itself with Jewish problems in the Roman Diaspora, had little relevance to the problems of the Jews in the Sassanid, or Babylonian, Diaspora.

Now the Jews in the Sassanid empire were faced with the same two choices the Jews in the Roman empire had been faced with after the destruction of the Temple. They could either seek an alternative way of life or somehow salvage the Torah as a workable document. Two Jews, Abba Arika and Mar Samuel, both former star pupils of Judah Hanasi, came up with a new idea they called Gemara based on the proposition that what was good for the Mishna goose was good for the Gemara gander.

Both Arika and Mar Samuel realized that the Diaspora Jews would have to produce their own rabbis and their own interpretations of the Torah to solve their problems. They could not expand the Mishna because they dared not defy Hanasi's ban. Their Gemara (from the Hebrew word "to supplement") was an ingenious solution to the dilemma. It clarified the Mishna in the same way that the Mishna clarified the Torah. As a new title always goes with a new job, the makers of the Gemara called themselves Amoraim.

Abba Arika was an aristocrat who moved in high Jewish and pagan social circles. In 227 C.E. he gave up his job as a superintendent of Jewish markets to found his famed academy at Sura, where he attracted the then-unheard-of enrollment of 1,200 students.

Arika's method of clarifying the Mishna was not only simple but farsighted, a method to be adopted 1,500 years later by the United States Supreme Court. In the same way the United States Supreme Court justices today listen to dissenting views and decide by majority vote which view can most logically be derived from the Constitution, so Arika took the text of Hanasi's Mishna, added the opinions of other experts, and subjected the result to the test of reason. A majority vote would decide which opinion would be the new law.

Arika, far ahead of his times, attempted to abolish marriage arrangements made for children without their consent, and threatened to excommunicate parents who would not send their children to school. When he died, he was eulogized by both Jews and pagans.

Mar Samuel (177–257 C.E.), the son of a wealthy merchant, was a famed eye specialist. When called to Jerusalem to cure an eye infection of Judah Hanasi, he fell under the spell of the great scholar and enrolled as a student. After graduation he stayed to help Hanasi edit the Mishna. Returning to Sassania, he was appointed head of an academy in Nehardea where he, too, taught the new Gemara.

Samuel, for those days, also had some bizarre ideas. One was that the courts should become guardians of orphans so they would not be thrown in the streets to shift for themselves. He also wanted to ban the widely held belief that an evil eye could cause death. He succeeded in the first but failed in the second.

Mar Samuel formulated three of the most important Diaspora survival laws still in effect today. He ordained that an oath taken in a non-Jewish court was as valid as an oath taken in a Jewish court; that in case of war a Jew must fight for the country in which he resides even if it means fighting against other Jews; and that the laws of the land in which Jews reside are their laws and had to be obeyed with but for three exceptions—Jews did not have to obey any law that forced them to murder, to commit incest, or to practice idolatry.

For two centuries (227–425 C.E.), the Amoraim guided Jewish life through the reefs of prosperity. They assured the Jews that the Gemara was not a departure from original Judaism but a natural outgrowth of the Torah through the Mishna.

But how long can one count on good luck? In the fifth century, the liberal government of the Sassanid empire was shattered by intolerant religious revolutions in which Jews and Christians were the victims. However, only the Jews were in double jeopardy. The reason was simple. Neither Mishna nor Gemara had been written down officially. The Amoraim were living libraries, carrying seven-hundred years of knowledge in their heads.

Each time an Amora was killed in a wave of excessive revolutionary zeal, the Jews were in danger of losing their Mishna and Gemara. Each time the head of an Amora was severed from his body, some 2,500,000 words of Mishna and Gemara, that had been crowding that brain, were lost.

Fearful that the Mishna and Gemara might some day rival the Torah as a final authority, the rabbis had forbidden that the Mishna and Gemara be written down. They could only be committed to memory. If the revolution kept on much longer, the danger was that, if not the Mishna, then certainly the Gemara, might become extinct.

Now or never was the time to defy the ban and commit both works to manuscript form. But who had the monumental knowledge to undertake such a task? It turned out to be a nineteen-year-old boy-wonder named Rav Ashi (352–427 C.E.) who bravely stepped in where wise men feared to tread. Perhaps his family's vast wealth and court connections helped give him the courage.

In retrospect, Rav Ashi's idea was as simple as it was bold. It was to combine in writing the Mishna and the Gemara into one indissoluble work, and then have it officially published. This combined work became the Talmud, from the Hebrew word meaning "learning."

For fifty-six years, Ashi labored on this project, often over the bitter objections of the same Jews who later came to revere the Talmud as much as the Torah itself. Around the year 500 C.E., the first official, inclusive written text of the Mishna with its commentary, the Gemara, was completed.

The Jews who had remained in Palestine also encountered new problems. They, too, fashioned a Talmud which became known as the Palestinian Talmud, to distinguish it from Rav Ashi's work, known as the Babylonian Talmud. But the Palestinian Talmud never achieved the influence and fame of the Babylonian.

The Talmud had been completed in the nick of time. It was the remedy which had been sent in advance of the next challenge waiting in the wings of history.

A new force was on the move in the seventh century. The Arab people had risen from the dust in the desert to march under the banner of a new prophet, Mohammed, proclaiming a new religion, Islam, in the name of a new god, Allah. The Sassanid empire was the first item on their agenda of conquest.

A new challenge for the Jews is at hand. Who or what will come to their rescue this time?

16

The Mail-Order Government

In the vastness of the Arabian peninsula, before the seventh century, dwelled two Arab peoples—the Quarish, mainly merchants living on trade and handicraft, and the Bedouins, eking out a miserable existence raising sheep and raiding caravans. They mingled only in the marketplaces where the Bedouins came to sell their sheep and stolen goods.

Both sects worshipped an assortment of objects like the moon, the stars, and stones. Both found human sacrifice effective in driving evil spirits away. Their highest form of worship, however, was reserved for a meteorite seven inches in diameter known as the Black Stone, housed in the Kaaba, a rectangular building in Mecca.

The greatest influence on these Arabs were the Jews who had settled in the Arabian peninsula as early as the days of King Solomon when his ships plied the seas in search of new markets. Subsequent Jewish migrations took place after the Assyrian and Babylonian wars, and after the revolts against Rome. The Jews founded the important merchant-city of Medina where they constituted the majority of the population. They also introduced the date palm tree which became to the Arabs what the potato became to the Irish, their chief staple food.

The Jew in Arabia was a fiery fighter, a crafty tradesman, and a skilled artisan who loved wine, women, and horses. Of Torah he knew little, and of Mishna and Gemara next to nothing. The Arabs, who had contempt for the Christians, admired the Jews for their learning, calling them "the people of the Book," referring to the Torah. In the same way that the Torah in its Greek translation prepared the way for Christianity, so the knowledge of the Torah among the Arabs prepared the way for Islam.

Mohammed, the founder of Islam, was born in 570 C.E. of humble parents. His father disappeared on the third day after the wedding and, at age six, Mohammed was orphaned when his mother died. An uncle taught him sheepherding but neglected to enrich his curriculum with other education, and Mohammed remained illiterate all his life.

Seeing little virtue in poverty, Mohammed married a rich, elderly widow who employed him as a camel driver for her caravans. His travels and business brought him in contact with the Jews and their religion. He brooded on the difference between the lofty monotheism of the Jews and the naive paganism of his people. One day the angel Gabriel, according to the Koran, the bible of the Muslims, appeared to Mohammed with the message that Allah had appointed him his prophet.

Mohammed's preaching was at first met with indifference. But when he dared attack the worship of the Black Stone, the tolerance for him turned to hostility. Fearing for his life, Mohammed fled to Medina, hoping the Jews would join his cause. When the Jews refused, he and his followers turned on them, looted their wealth, and used it to equip an army. The Arabs in Mecca, upon beholding Mohammed's new army, quickly recognized the superiority of Allah over the Black Stone. Within two years Mohammed was master of the entire peninsula.

Mohammed's death in 632 C.E. did not stop his conquering armies. Without pretending to be harbingers of peace, the Arabs came with naked scimitars. Within five decades they had conquered the water and land from the Indian Ocean to the Mediterranean Sea. In 711 C.E., a former slave named Tariq, led a mixed force of Arabs, Moors, and Berbers across the Straits of Gibraltar, conquering Spain after a four-year campaign. The Arab streak of luck was halted in 732 C.E. at Tours, France, by Charles Martel, the mayor of the palace, and grandfather of Emperor Charlemagne.

And thus it came about that the Jews again found themselves in a new empire, in a new civilization, in a new religion—and up to their chins in new problems.

The Jews reacted spontaneously and did what by now came naturally. They fired the old scriptwriters and hired a new set of specialists. As with the challenge of Hellenism, the Jews did not reject the Islamic society, but joined it. Arabic became their mother tongue. They entered new, unheard-of professions for Jews. Not only did they become famed Talmudists, doctors, lawyers, and businessmen, but they also became famed philosophers, mathematicians, astronomers, diplomats, grammarians, and poets, contributing greatly to Islamic civilization.

Empire-makers are always faced with the problem of what to do with unassimilable elements in conquered territories. This was also the case with the Islamic empire carved out of Sassanid, Byzantine, and Roman leftovers. Pagans had no problems; they simply exchanged one set of gods and beliefs for another on the theory that to the victor belonged the spoils and religious affiliations. The problem for the Arabs was not the pagan Iranians, Egyptians, Moroccans, Tunisians and Algerians; they were converted to Islam, and they have stayed within Islam to this day. The problem was the Christians and Jews who would not convert.

After an initial policy of hostility toward Jews and Christians, the Arabs permitted them to hang on to their religious "superstitions" provided they paid a special tax. But whereas the Jews, in the main, were recognized as men of learning—the people of the Book—the Arabs took a dimmer view of the Christians.

The special contempt the Arabs held for the Christians expressed itself in the Pact of Omar, enacted in 637 C.E. after Christian Syria and Palestine fell into Muslim hands. Though the pact is presumed by some scholars to also apply to Jews, the Jews are not referred to by name in it. The pact specifies among other things that Christians could not display crosses on churches or in public places; that they had to wear distinctive dress to identify themselves as Christians; that they could not convert Muslims to Christianity; and so on. These restrictions have a familiar ring; they are the same kinds of laws that Christians were to apply to the Jews in Europe five centuries later.

A remarkable aspect of this Christian sojourn in Arab lands was that whereas the Jews produced a golden age of science and literature and rose to posts of eminence, the Christians achieved little of note in their five-century stay in Arab lands. Most of the Christians integrated into Muslim society and disappeared as Christians, whereas the Jews survived as Jews.

We have by this time seen how Jewish history alternates between stretches of bad times followed by periods of good times. The periods of persecution are usually short, less than five decades in duration. The periods of tolerance stretch from two to five centuries. Some historians have a habit of concentrating on the short intervals of persecution rather than on the achievements during the far longer intervals of tolerance. The fact is that the centuries from Abraham to Mohammed were full of injustice for everybody. But the Jews were the only survivors from that starting line back in 2000 B.C.E., and thus have had a longer time than any other people to acquire more of the injustices.

All of the great ages and ideas of the Jewish people occurred during good times not bad. The Torah was given to the Jews not when they were slaves in Egypt, but after they were freed. The Mishna was born in the permissive period of the Greco-Roman world. The Gemara bloomed in the tolerant society of the Sassanid empire. And the Talmud flourished in the equally tolerant Islamic period.

The Arabs opted for the Jewish policies of the Sassanids. They retained the office of the Exilarch with its former privileges. To it they added another, the position of the Gaon, his eminence, who was none other than the head of one of the two leading Talmudic yeshivas.

The Exilarch, especially, was held in great esteem not only by the Jews but by the Muslim rulers. Benjamin of Tudela in Spain, who visited Baghdad in the twelfth century, has left us a report of the homage paid to the Exilarch when the Exilarch went to visit the caliph. He wrote: "Horsemen escort him and heralds proclaim, 'Make way for the son of David.'

He is mounted on a horse and is attired in silk and embroidery . . . . He appears before the Caliph and kisses his hands, and the Caliph rises and places him on the throne which Mohammed ordered to be made in his honor."*

The Geonim wrote no Gemara. Instead they interpreted the Talmud. The office of the Gaon was flooded with mail from Jews asking his eminence what the Jewish response should be to specific problems.

The Geonim, after duly deliberating the questions in a manner reminiscent of United States Supreme Court deliberations, would send to the questioners responses based on the Talmud. The Geonim in effect created a "mail-order government" of questions and answers, called the Responsa. Though this Responsa literature did not become part of the Talmud, it did become an additional basis for future decisions in other situations.

The main thrust of Geonic thinking tended to be liberal. So, for instance, the Talmudists ruled that a laborer's salary could not be stopped because of illness. Limits were set on working hours, and guilds were given the right to protect wages. Women and children could not be exploited.

However, workers had responsibilities too under this Talmudic law. They had to have the skills necessary for the job, and they were held responsible for damages resulting from proven inefficiency or sabotage. Luxuries could be sold at any price. But in bad times, the price of grain and other necessities could be fixed to prevent speculation and hardship.

Let us take one Torah law and see how it was amplified and expanded into a system of ethics. The Torah forbids the eating of carrion. But what is carrion? The Talmudists based their answer not on what was profitable but on what was moral. They declared that the meat of an animal which had died in pain was carrion and hence forbidden to be eaten. But how could one determine if an animal had died in pain or not? This led to the question of humane slaughter. The answer: Death, must be instantaneous, caused by one cut with a sharp, unblemished knife across the jugular vein and carotid artery.

For centuries, Jews have been aghast at the inhumane slaughtering methods of their non-Jewish neighbors who killed animals in any way they pleased. The medieval Christians thought the Jews rejected their meat because it wasn't good enough for them. To explain to a ninth-century Christian that the reason a Jew could not eat the meat was because the slaughtered cow had a right to die without pain would have meant to invite either laughter or death. After all, if few human beings in medieval times had any rights, it stood to reason, to the Christian mind, that no animal had any rights either.

Not until the twentieth century did the Western world catch up with the Jewish standards. And not until the 1920s were the first slaughtering laws enacted in the United States. But the practice of forcing premature

*From *The Jew in the Medieval World*, by Jacob R. Marcus.

birth in animals in order to obtain the soft skin of the preborn young, which the Talmud forbade a thousand years ago, is still practiced today in countries such as Iran and France, where that soft skin is used to make fine hats and gloves.

The three-and-a-half-century rule (700–1050 C.E.) of the Geonim produced many outstanding Talmudists, but three were most famed. They were the blind internationalist, Yehudai ben Nahman (Gaon 750–4 C.E.), the intolerant liberal, Saadia (882–942 C.E.) and the tolerant conservative, Hai (939–1038 C.E.).

Despite his blindness, his advanced age of eighty, and his brief four-year term in office, Yehudai ben Nahman was the first to unite the Jews living on three continents into one Jewish community. His book *Decided Laws* was the first to deal with international aspects of property rights, travel, and inheritance laws. It also explored the field of maritime law with such relevance that centuries later the renowned Dutch jurist, Hugo Grotius (1583–1645), used many of Yehudai's opinions in his works on international maritime law.

Two views exist of Saadia—that of a saint with nary an evil thought in his angelic life, and that of a Machiavellian conspirator clawing his way to the top with cunning and his father-in-law's money.

Saadia, born in a small-town slum in Egypt, was a genius who left his radical imprint on Judaism. At the age of twenty, he published a Hebrew lexicon, then translated the entire Torah into Arabic. His greatest contribution was his rationalist interpretation of the Talmud, and filling his Responsa with common sense. He died in 942 C.E. of melancholia, a cluster of symptoms known today as schizophrenia.

Hai was born in Baghdad where he attended the most prestigious schools. Fluent in Hebrew, Arabic, and Persian, he was an Orthodox Jew who did not let his orthodoxy interfere with his rationalism. His vast Responsa was modern; his famed work *Buying and Selling*—tractates on the international aspects of commerce, interest, and contracts—was so cogent that many of his tractates are still relevant to international law today.

All this activity by the Geonim did not take place in a vacuum. Their Responsa was much needed to help bridge the change from an agrarian society to the emerging new capitalist society. The fact was that the Jews had become famed international merchants whose ships sailed the seas from the Atlantic to the Pacific, dominating maritime commerce for three centuries (800–1100 C.E.), and new laws were needed to guide them.

Known as Radanites, these Jewish merchants reached China as early as 900 C.E. via two main routes, one by sea, the other by land. The land route the Jews had blazed was followed in the main by Marco Polo, who testified to the strong commercial presence of the Jews in China.

The reason for this dominance in the world of commerce was two-fold. Jews living in the cities around the Mediterranean had business connections from Baghdad to Cordoba. They spoke not only Arabic, Persian, Greek, and Spanish, but also the languagues of the Franks, the Arab collective term for the French, Italians, and Germans. Thus, with one foot in the Islamic empire and the other in Christian Europe, the Jews were able to infuse Arab capitalism into Europe's feudal arteries.

The second reason was perhaps even more important. In the Talmud the Jews had an international law which Jews, Arabs, and Christians had learned to rely upon. No one hesitated to accept the promissory note of a Jew, because all knew that a Talmudic court would enforce its payment. This freed the Jewish merchants from the necessity of carrying huge quantities of gold to settle debts and to pay for goods with cash on the barrelhead. Carrying gold was always an invitation to be robbed or killed.

The tenth century was a watershed period in Jewish history. It funneled the Jews from the East to West, from an Oriental to a European mode of thinking. This was brought about in part by a breakup of the Islamic world and in part by a remarkable Jewish religious revolt in the eighth century, which had unanticipated consequences in the tenth century.

17

The Karaite Revolt

In the eighth century C.E. a religious schism split Jewish ranks into a rebellion against the Talmud. This heresy was Karaism, from the Hebrew word Karah, literally meaning "to read." Figuratively, however, it stands for "reading the Torah." Hence the Karaite revolt was a strife of Torahism versus Talmudism.

The leader of this revolt was Anan ben David (740–800 C.E.), whose life runs counter to the tradition of a humble origin for a Jewish religious leader. Anan began right at the top as a wealthy aristocrat of royal lineage, the heir to the chair of the Exilarch.

There are two versions of what happened. One presents Anan ben David as a rebel against Talmudism because his less brilliant brother was appointed Exilarch instead of him. In revenge, Anan set out deliberately to create a schism in Judaism by falsely claiming that the Prophet Elijah had commanded him to abolish the Talmud.

The other view presents Anan as a pious man who, upon being elected Exilarch, wanted to restore the Torah to its former eminence. But the Jewish establishment, fearing him, asked the caliph to have him put to death for heresy. Anan pleaded that he had a different religion and that he was Exilarch of the Jews of this different sect. The caliph set him free to preach his doctrine of the supremacy of the Torah over the Talmud.

On the surface, Karaism appears to be a simple grass-roots revolt against the Talmud. In the main, the Karaites rejected anything the Talmud said. Most Talmudic dietary rules and the use of phylacteries, for example, were abolished. Customs that they thought had no basis in reason were annulled. Curiously enough, like Christian Scientists today, the Karaites also foreswore medicine and did not consult physicians because Scripture says "I am the Lord that healeth thee."

Some historians see Karaism as more than a revolt against the Talmud. They see the Karaites as pious Jews who viewed Talmudic decisions as a curtain between the people and the Torah. These historians see Karaism as the first reform movement in Judaism.

The Karaites were also the forerunners of modern Zionism. Talmudic Judaism had become exile-oriented, gearing the Talmud for survival in a permanent Diaspora.

The Karaites rejected the idea that the Diaspora was a permanent ingredient in Jewish destiny. They wanted an immediate return to Palestine, not under the leadership of a messiah but through their own efforts. Though the crown of a messiah was thrust several times upon Anan ben David by his followers, he threw it off each time. He led his followers to Palestine, settling in Jerusalem where he and his successors were known as patriarchs.

At first, the Talmudists thought that, if ignored, Karaism would go away. When it did not, they resorted to invective and bans, to no avail. What eventually doomed the Karaites was a Talmudist turned philosopher —Saadia, the Gaon in Baghdad. He was the first to acknowledge that there was much that was valid in the aspirations of the Karaites. His first move was to open the Talmud to more liberal thinking. Then he translated the Torah into Arabic so that the Arab-speaking Jews, who no longer understood Hebrew, would not have to depend on the Karaites to learn what the Torah said. He also asserted the primacy of Hebrew in the survival of the Jews and undertook to write the first Hebrew lexicon. Then, and only then, did Saadia pen a series of devastating articles against the Karaites.

As a force in Judaism, Karaism lasted four centuries. What finally did it in was not Saadia's brilliance, but the sweep of current events. For four centuries (800–1200 C.E.), the Karaites flourished in Palestine, again making Jerusalem a lively Jewish intellectual center. In 1060 C.E., the Seljuk Turks captured Jerusalem; thirty years later they were ousted by the Arabs, and in 1099 the Crusaders wrested the city from the Saracens. The Crusaders slaughtered all civilians—Arabs, Turks, and Jews—and the Karaite movement in Palestine collapsed. By the fourteenth century, the Karaites had vanished as a force in Jewish history. Today there are only about ten thousand Karaites, mostly in Israel and Lithuania.

But the Karaite revolt had not been in vain. It prevented Talmudism from becoming static, and it set Judaism on a new course. As the eastern sector of the Islamic empire, anchored in Baghdad, was crumbling under the relentless invasions of barbarians from the heartland of Asia, the Jews fled West. Though some went to Christian Europe, most went to Moorish Spain. Among those who fled were not only conservative Talmudists but also the intellectual heirs of Saadia's liberal ideas.

And thus it came about that the Jewish intellectual reawakening did not take place in Islam East, the eastern half of the Islamic empire, as one might have suspected, but in Islam West, the western sector of the Islamic empire, in Moorish Spain.

18

The Land of
Three Religions
and One Bedroom

Spain's history is shrouded in obscurity until the fourth century B.C.E., when the Semitic Carthaginians brought that peninsula its first civilization. The Romans arrived two centuries later. Soon thereafter came the Jews as ambassadors, businessmen, refugees, and slaves, in that order, reflecting their changing political status.

The first of the barbarian invaders to hit the Iberian peninsula were the Vandals whose vengeful rule was mercifully brief. The Christian Visigoths, who supplanted them (412 C.E.) brought an end to Jewish tranquility. With the zeal of recent converts themselves, the Visigoths forcibly converted almost all of Spain's fifty thousand Jews to Christianity.

The Moors, after their invasion of Spain in 711 C.E., put an end to the Christian persecution by substituting their own. But after a few decades, the Moors lost their zeal, and instituted a policy of indifference toward non-believers, provided they paid a non-believer tax.

The subsequent five-hundred-year rule of the Muslims (700–1200 C.E.) was most tolerant for those days. There emerged what has been called a Spain of three religions and one bedroom," where Jews, Christians, and Muslims shared a brilliant civilization that blended religions, cultures, and bloodlines.

Spain, under Arab rule, became the most civilized country in the world. The Jews soared to the highest posts in the land. They became viziers, kissing cousins to royalty, and avant-garde members in the aristocratic elite. Cordoba, saturated with Jews, became the most beautiful and vivacious city on the continent, a city famed for her palaces and magnificent libraries.

The Jews in Spain were numerous, wealthy, and influential, but they were not known for scholarship until after the eleventh century, after the Jews in Spain were enriched with Jewish refugees from the Eastern Arab countries. The three centuries from 1000 to 1300 C.E., during which the Jews in Spain produced a succession of brilliant Talmudists, philosophers, scientists, grammarians, and poets, have become known as the Golden Age in Spain.

Though the seeds for that intellectual revolution were not sown until after 1000 C.E., the soil had been mulched as early as 800 C.E. Wars produce strange bedfellows and queer byproducts. As a consequence of the Arab victories, it befell Jews as well as Christians to rescue Greek literary and scientific works for the Arabs.

The early Christians had no use for the writings of the heathen Greeks. The church nevertheless had stored them for safe keeping in libraries and monasteries to prevent their destruction by invading barbarians. For five centuries these manuscripts and codices in Greek, and in Syrian translations, were forgotten. But, with their conquest of territories formerly held by the Christians, the Arabs rediscovered them. They asked the Jews —the cosmopolitans of that age who collectively spoke Hebrew, Latin, Greek, Syriac and Arabic—to translate these works into Arabic. This was the first introduction of the world of the Greeks to the Arabs.

When the enlightened crowned heads of Europe heard of these Greek treasures, they invited the Jews to come to their realms to translate the works of the Greeks and the Arabs, as well as their own Hebrew literature, into Latin. One of the first of these Jewish intellectuals imported by the rulers of Europe was ibn Daud who not only translated Greek, Arabic, and Hebrew literature into Latin but also introduced Arabic numerals, the concept of zero, and Euclid's Elements into the mainstream of European science. Soon thereafter, Jewish, Arab, and Christian scholars sat side by side in libraries and monasteries, translating Plato and Aristotle, Arab mathematicians and scientists, Jewish philosophers and astronomers, into Latin, the language of the Holy Roman Church; into Hebrew, the holy language of the Jews; and into Arabic, the everyday language of the Muslims and Jews. This represented the first rays of light in Europe's dark age.

In these three centuries, Jews prominent in astronomy, mathematics, linguistics, geography, and philosophy were as numerous as the stars in heaven. The reason one seldom hears of them is that Western civilization has been so busy extolling the Greeks that Jews and Arabs have as yet not received full credit for their contributions. Space permits us to choose only a few random examples.

Abraham Zacuto, astronomer to the kings of Spain and Portugal, was famed for his astronomical tables which were used by Columbus and Vasco da Gama. Levi ben Gershon invented the quadrant known as Jacob's staff, so essential to the explorers of the New World. He was also the father of modern trigonometry, not Johann Muller who stole those ideas and published them as his own.

Dunash ibn Labrit was the first grammarian to develop the theory of the three-letter root of Hebrew and all Semitic language. Abraham bar

Hiyyah, a philosopher and scientist, wrote famed works on geography and astronomy, and predicted the arrival of the Jewish messiah in 1358.

Science 'and philosophy also invaded the minds of the Talmudists themselves. Solomon ibn Adret, known as the Rabbi of Spain, opposed messiahs, mystics, and the study of science for Jews under thirty. David Kimhi, grammarian and philologist, wrote Bible commentaries with such insight that Christian scholars used them as source material in their translations of the Bible into European languages.

However, these three centuries, so rich in Jewish intellectual creativity, also caused a schism. When one opens a Pandora's box, one never knows what will come out. In this case a split between faith and reason developed. The practical effect was that, for the first time, Judaism was forced to justify itself. Was Judaism valid or not?

To make matters worse, Judaism was beset with the success of the two new religions, Christianity and Islam. Whereas each of them had become a world religion, Judaism had been rejected by the world. The question asked was, "If Judaism is such a wonderful religion, how come no one else wants it?"

There was, however, a rebuttal which skillfully bypassed the two horns of this dilemma. It was the Aristotelian argument that true wisdom was for intellectuals only and could not be appreciated by the masses. But did this apply to Judaism? Was it an elitist religion reserved only for intellectuals? Was this the image the Jews wished to project of their religion?

The ideas of three Spanish-Jewish scholars illustrate this agonizing dilemna into which the Jews had been placed by the triumph of science and philosophy on the one hand, and the successes of Christianity and Islam on the other. Today, this same dilemma also confronts Christianity and Islam as science and new ideologies compete with faith.

The three philosophers who tried to come to grips with the problem were Judah Halevi (1075–1141 C.E.), the romantic poet of the Diaspora who yearned to rehabilitate Judaism in the eyes of the world; Moses Maimonides (1135–1204 C.E.), the pro-Aristotelian Talmudist who wanted to justify Judaism in the eyes of the intellectuals; and Hasdai Crescas (1340–1410 C.E.), the anti-Aristotelian rabbi who, in wanting to defend Judaism against the skeptics, paved a path for the skeptic philosophers.

Judah Halevi, born to wealth, abandoned his family and a successful career in medicine for the life of a vagabond. He hitchhiked to Cordoba, there to dedicate his life to poetry. He scandalized the purists by daring to express, in sacred Hebrew, passions not penned in that language since King Solomon's Song of Songs. But he soon gave up his life of revelry to become a troubador of God.

Halevi was troubled by the fact the Judaism had been rejected by the world. He came up with a unique conclusion: Judaism had never had a chance to be freely chosen by the people of the world. Christianity and

Islam, he held, had been foisted on the people by force. In a free choice, he averred, the people would choose Judaism. This is the theme of his most famed work, *Ha-Kuzari,* meaning the Khazars.

The Khazars, a Tartaric people living in the land wedged between the Black Sea and Caspian Sea, in what is now Southern Russia, are of special interest to the Jews becuase about the year 786 C.E. their King Bulan and his nobles converted to Judaism. For two-and-a-half centuries the Jewish Khazars were feared by their neighbors who paid them a sizable annual tribute. This state of affairs came to an end in 969 C.E. when Duke Sviatoslav of Kiev made war on the Khazars and converted them to Christianity.

The conversion of King Bulan to Judaism is the central theme in Halevi's work. The king, shopping around for a new religion, listens to a Muslim and a Christian presenting views on their respective religions. When both refer to Judaism as the "Father religion," Bulan sends for a Jewish scholar, who presents Judaism as a historic event in which God gave his Torah openly to all Jews. Bulan chooses Judaism. This to Halevi proves the point that, if given equal time, Judaism would become the choice of the people of all nations.

As for Halevi himself, there is fulfillment only in Jerusalem. He sets out on a pilgrimage to the Holy Land, but makes it only as far as Damascus. Here history loses track of him.

Maimonides takes up the opposite of Halevi's theme. Born in Cordoba to a distinguished family of financiers, statesmen, and scholars, he had to flee his hometown as fanatic Muslim sects instituted a policy of persecuting Jews and Christians. He eventually settled in Cairo, where he became Egypt's most famed physician.

In these troubled times, Maimonides undertook to codify the entire Talmud into one definitive work to serve the Jews as a guide for survival. With unabashed snobbery he wrote in the introduction, "This work will assemble the entire Oral Law from the days of Moses to the completion of the Talmud. . . . For this reason I have called it *The Second Torah.*" He then adds, with commendable confidence, "One needs only to read the Torah first, then study my book to learn the entire Oral Law." And he was right.

The publication of *The Second Torah* stunned the fundamentalist Jews who could not believe that anyone would dare to introduce Greek philosophy into their Holy Book. A shower of abuse was heaped on this self-styled Moses who presumed to hand down a second Torah as though he had received it personally from God in Cairo. Within a century, however, he became the most revered Talmudist.

Malmonides was also the author of *A Guide to the Perplexed,* in which he presented Judaism as a rational philosophy. This interpretation would have bewildered Moses of Sinai, who certainly did not have Aristotle in mind when he handed down the law. It also enraged the Jews of

France who denounced the guide to the French church. In 1238 C.E. an obliging church burned all available copies.

Hasdai Crescas, born in Barcelona, moved in royal circles. As a youth he received a prison sentence for an alleged participation in the assassination of a Jewish friend of the king of Castile. After his release from prison, Crescas became the chief rabbi of Saragossa. Offended that Maimonides had permitted Aristotelian ideas to creep into the Talmud, he set out to downgrade Maimonides by attacking the philosophy of Aristotle. He succeeded so brilliantly that he undermined the entire medieval philosophical structure based on Aristotle. Thus the rabbi who wanted Judaism to steer away from science and philosophy, paved the path for Descartes and Spinoza and the rule of science.

Even before the death of Hasdai Crescas, the Jewish Golden Age in Moorish Spain had come to an end. Fierce nomadic and Arab tribes rode across North Africa, invading the Iberian peninsula. Moorish Spain disintegrated into petty caliphates and emirates, each ruled by its own war lords. The tide of the Reconquista (1000–1500 C.E.)—as the five-century Christian struggle to regain Spain from the Moors was called—pushed the Muslims further and further south, and finally across the Strait of Gibraltar back into Africa. By 1400 C.E. Spain was all but Christian again. As Islamic lands sank into cultural oblivion, a new age was dawning for Europe. And for the Jews.

In retrospect, the Jews had not fared too badly for the first thousand years of their exile, considering that scores of other nations in that same millenium had lost kith, kin, and country. For a thousand years the Jews had lived in the expanding societies of the Parthian, Sassanid, and Islamic empires; they had lived in a world where scholars were admired; they had mingled with aristocrats and flirted with the sciences. They had lived in a world which generally tolerated the Jews but despised the Christians.

Now, in the tenth century, history began to transplant the Jews from the land of the Arabs to Christian Europe. It was a totally new scene. Popes replaced caliphs. Bishops replaced imams. Cathedrals took the place of mosques. And instead of minarets in every marketplace, there was a cross with Jesus nailed to it wherever church bells chimed.

Will the Jews be able to survive this awesome challenge on all fronts —cultural, social, economic, religious? Can a Babylonian Talmud be of help on a Christian continent? If the Jews ever needed help, they needed it now.

PART II

The Four Adventures in Christian Europe

(500–2000 C.E.)

The Medieval church hoped to convert the Jews by religious disputations. It was like a game of "Russian roulette"—if the Jewish team could not disprove Christian charges, there was the threat of forcible conversion; if it trumped Christian scholarship it ran the risk of being put to death. Here three Christians and three Jews get set for a duel with Gospel and Decalogue.

The First Adventure

(500–1100 C.E.)

The Jews, after surviving the devastation of barbarian invaders become, to their vast surprise, the symbolic servants of the king and the only non-Christian people in Christian Europe protected by the church and granted unheard-of freedoms for the common man in feudal Europe.

Until the nineteenth century, the Jews poured all their artistic creativity into the making of religious artifacts and designing illuminated bible manuscripts—as exemplified by this illumination from the Flemish period, thirteenth century.

19

Background to Danger

The fifteen-hundred-year-long path Jewish history took in Western civilization is as intricate as the design in an oriental tapestry. If we trace only one strand of events at a time, we get lost in a succession of meaningless episodes. But, if we pursue clusters of events, then we can see meaningful relationships between Christian and Jewish history. As heresies against the Church increase, persecution against the Jews also increases. As democratic revolutions sweep Europe, the walls of the ghetto crumble. As European nationalism begets anti-Semitism, it also begets Zionism.

Four distinct Jewish adventures are woven in the overall design of Jewish history in Christian Europe. The First Adventure is the amazing survival of the Jews from the fall of the Roman empire to the first Crusade (600–1100 C.E.). It is a five-century gamble, with Jewish survival at stake at each spin of the wheel.

The Second Adventure spans the five centuries from the first Crusade to the century of the Reformation (1100–1600 C.E.). In this adventure, history plays a cruel joke on the Jews. After first clothing them in the silks of the Renaissance, it callously disrobes them of this finery and garbs them instead in demeaning ghetto caftans.

The Third Adventure is an inglorious chapter in Christian history and a testament to the indomitable spirit of the Jews. It is the story of survival against all odds in a three-century-long imprisonment (1550–1850 C.E.) by the Christians in the dank ghettos of Europe.

The Fourth Adventure is the modern age itself (from 1800 until today). It is a colorful concerto in three distinct movements: the first, a spirited balletto celebrating the Jewish emancipation from the ghettos; the second, a dirge capturing the horrors of the concentration camps "when Israel's soul drifted as smoke" through the chimneys of German barbarism; and the third, a triumphant scherzo heralding the creation of the state of Israel.

20
The Invaders

The Roman empire weakened dramatically in the fourth century. After that it was downhill for Rome until the empire petered out in the sixth century.

The decline of Rome began in China, in the early third century C.E., when the Chinese expelled hundreds of thousands of nomadic Huns, squatting on China's borders, with the warning not to come back. This expulsion set in motion a gigantic movement of people across Asia into Europe.

When the Huns crossed the Ural Mountains into the plains of Russia, they ran into the Ostrogoths whom the Huns drove like a herd of pigs into Europe. The Ostrogoths ran into a second lineup of other barbarians strung along a line from the Baltic Sea to the Black Sea, whom they in turn drove across Europe to the Atlantic. Thus, there were three major waves of barbarians invading Europe.

Each new wave took turns sacking Rome, and Rome could stand only so many sackings. Rome, which had begun the fourth century with one million people, ended the sixth century with less than fifty thousand. Barbarians now marched under the triumphal Arch of Titus.

By the end of the seventh century, the damage had been completed. The spawn of the invaders covered the entire European continent. Visigoths had overrun Spain; Ostrogoths had conquered Italy; Franks had vanquished France. Saxons and Huns had taken possession of Germany. England was added in the eleventh century when William the Conqueror, the illegitimate son of the French Duke of Normandy and a tanner's daughter, invaded that island and annexed it.

The history of France begins in the fifth century with a Magyar chief named Clovis, who unified the country by terror. Europe, however, had to wait another three centuries for Charlemagne (771–814 C.E.) to civilize the continent. Six feet tall, pitiless, arrogant, and illiterate, Charlemagne was a constant winner of wars who united the future France, Germany, and Italy into one Frankish empire.

Wherever Charlemagne went, he converted pagans to Christianity, never taking no for an answer, except from the Jews. He did, however have trouble with his racial cousins, the pagan Saxons, who preferred the worship of a horse's skull nailed to a tree to that of Jesus nailed to a cross.

If anyone wonders where the Jews were during these centuries of invasion, the answer is, right there, in the midst of it. That the Jews survived this general devastation in remarkably good shape was in itself an amazing achievement.

The Jews are, all too often, portrayed during these invasion centuries as suffering lambs, prey to anti-Semitic wolves. What we tend to forget is that this was an age of calamity for everyone—Jews, Christians, and pagans. The invading barbarians never inquired into the religious affiliations of those they killed. If Jews expected the invaders merely to ask them to step aside because they were Jews, then they expected too much. The invading hordes from the East raped and killed Jews, Christians, and pagans impartially.

Jews who had arrived in Rome as early as the first and second century C.E., were there in ample time to be raped and killed in the three seccessive sackings of Rome. Jews who had settled in Spain at the dawn of the Common Era were there on cue to be greeted and killed by Vandals and Visigoths. And having arrived in Germany and southern France in the second century C.E., they were on hand to be decimated along with the rest of the population by an assortment of invading Franks, Saxons, and Huns.

Thus, by the seventh century, those Jews who had survived, constituted an elite segment to whom the Darwinian term "survival of the fittest" could be aptly applied.

Not only did the Jews have the good luck to survive the invasions without terminal damage, but they also had the additional luck to come to the attention of the new rulers of Europe as people of enterprise.

Theodoric the Great of Italy set the future pattern. As early as the sixth century C.E., he invited the Jews to come to his capital in Ravenna, to Rome, Venice, Milan, to spark commercial activity and help bring prosperity to his realm. Other crowned heads of Europe followed his lead.

And, as if that was not enough, the church added yet one more blessing. At this point in history, it had not yet given the Jews an ultimatum to convert to Christianity. Jews were permitted to stay non-Christian at a time when no one else was granted such a concession.

But why was everybody so good to the Jews? Herein lies an incredible tale.

21

The Great Goof

Two general misconceptions are held by many about the Jews during the Middle Ages—that they lived in ghettos and that they were nothing but peddlers and grubby moneylenders. Neither was the case.

Until the fourteenth century, the Jews were generally free to live wherever they chose, and were far from being pitiful creatures. They had it better, in fact, than the majority of the Christian population.

As these assertions run counter to generally held beliefs, let us examine the facts.

By the eighth century C.E., a political system known as feudalism had settled over Europe. It consisted of three social classes, or estates—the nobles who did the fighting, the priests who did the praying, and the serfs who comprised ninety-five percent of the population and did the work. Their lot was not a happy one.

The serf was a slave in all but name. Though the plot of land he tilled belonged to him technically, it nevertheless was controlled by the lord of the manor. A serf could not travel further than one day from his lord's estate, and he could be sold with the land. He could own only wooden dishes, and was permitted but one wooden spoon for the entire family. Everything he wore, ate, or used was regulated by his lord to whom he paid a crippling percentage of everything he produced. Lord and serf usually had but two things in common—they were equally illiterate and equally superstitious.

But the devisers of the feudal system had left out something. They had forgotten to provide for a middle class of tradesmen, businessmen, bankers, and professionals. The Christians needed them to fuel their economy, to keep the three estates in working order. So as not to upset the system and cause the collapse of the feudal order, the nobles decided to import Jews to serve as such a middle class.

And so it came about that while the Christian lords were busy pushing each other out of saddles in tournaments, while priests were busy praying for everyone's soul, while serfs were busy tilling the soil from sunup to sundown, the Jews became the scholars, physicians, bankers, and merchants of feudal Europe. They established vast networks of international enterprise with headquarters in Baghdad, Alexandria, Tangiers, Aachen, Marseilles, joining the Radanites in extending their business activities to India and China.

The crowned heads of Europe followed the pattern set by Theodoric the Great. Emperor Charlemagne, for instance, offered the Jews every inducement to entice them into his kingdom. He needed literate Jews as bankers, physicians, and diplomats. He granted the Jews land for settlement and charters for special privileges.

Thus, before accepting these invitations, the Jews were able to demand, and receive, land grants to establish their own Jewish quarters so they could live close to synagogue and cemetery. Often, too, they were granted city charters and the right to elect their own officials. In no sense of the word did these Jewish quarters constitute ghettos. They were voluntary Jewish neighborhoods into which, or out of which, the Jews could move at will.

It has been pointed out that these freedoms of the Jews were only paper freedoms, that actually the Jews were nothing but *servi camera*; that is, "servants of the king." This is absolutely true. The Jews were indeed the servants of the king, but it was this very fact that gave them the freedoms they had.

To keep his realm intact, the feudal king or lord demanded an oath of loyalty in the name of Jesus from all his subjects. As the Jews refused to take such an oath for religious reasons, they were exempted from doing so. Instead they swore loyalty in the name of the king, and thus they became servants of the king instead of subjects of Jesus.

But this did not enslave the Jews to the king. Instead it freed them from the feudal restrictions binding on the serfs. Along with nobles and high-ranking clergy, the Jews had the right to move about freely on horse or in carriage, to be able to carry out their business transactions.

As these were dangerous times to travel, the Jews were also given the same right as the nobles to carry arms to defend themselves. Few dared to rob a Jewish travelling merchant, for doing so would be like robbing the king.

There were of course exceptions, as we shall note later. But we must remember that we are dealing with an entire continent over a period of five centuries. Many injustices can be found in so vast a space over such a long span of time. By and large, however, Jews during the High Middle Ages had it better than ninety-five percent of the population, enjoying privileges the serfs did not have.

But there was to be a day of reckoning. The serfs would rebel against their condition, overthrow the feudal state, displace their feudal lords, swarm the cities, expel the Jews, and go into business for themselves.

But that was not until later. Meanwhile, let us explore the challenges and responses of the Jews in their first adventure in Christian lands.

22

The Turning of the Screw

No one has ever tried so persistently to convert a people from one faith to another as did the Christians in their efforts to convert the Jews. As it turned out, this was a blessing, for otherwise the Jews might have been annihilated along with all other non-Christian people in Europe.

It had taken the church one thousand years—from about 300 to 1300 C.E.—to establish Christianity in Europe with Bible and sword, mostly with sword. The church gave everyone two choices—conversion or death. The resulting slaughter in the name of Jesus was monumental. By 1300, everyone in Christian Europe was either Christian or dead, except one people—the Jews. They were the only people still alive on the continent who were not Christian.

Why had the Jews not been exterminated in the same way all other non-Christian people on the continent had been when they refused to accept Christianity? The Jews were, after all, the most vulnerable people in Europe. They had no armies and no country of their own.

The paradoxical answer is the church did not want to kill the Jews. In fact, the Church protected them from being killed by overzealous lords and priests. Again, the question is why?

The answer does not make much sense today, but it did then. Europe's feudal society was a religious one. It was important to the church to convert the Jews to Christianity because this would give the church greater credibility. Otherwise, how could the church claim that Christianity was the fulfillment of the Old Testament if the Jews did not acknowledge it?

Thus in the first ten centuries of Christianity, every conciliation was held out to the Jews to induce them to convert. When they steadfastly refused, it placed the church in a dilemma. What should it do—have the Jews killed, or continue to wait patiently for the Jews to come around?

96

The church chose to wait. However, to hasten the day of conversion, the church began to pass a series of laws against the Jews that made it uncomfortable to be Jewish. It began applying the same laws against the Jews that the Arab Pact of Omar had applied against the Christians long before. These laws enacted by the Christians cannot be judged by today's standards of democracy since democracy did not exist at that time.

None of the laws was aimed at exterminating the Jews, only to nudge them into Christianity by making it progressively more uncomfortable to remain Jewish. Century after century the discrimination continued. The Jews, nevertheless adjusted their lives to each successive law, and remained Jewish.

Until the twelfth century c.e., Jews and Christians lived side by side without too much hostility, because these laws functioned more in the breach than in the observance. From the decree of Pope Gregory the Great (591 c.e.) forbidding the forcible conversion of Jews, to the Fourth Lateran Council (1215 c.e.) enacting special distinctive dress for Jews to single them out as non-Christians, the Jews lived for these centuries in comparative freedom and prosperity. True enough, anti-Jewish incidents did occur, but these were usually not sponsored by pope or emperor. By and large, few Jews during these five centuries would have willingly traded their standard of living and way of life for that of a Christian serf.

In the twelfth century this general tranquility was shattered by the Crusades. With them began an era of active hostility toward the Jews.

The persecution of the Jews underwent three distinct chronological phases; each more sinister than the one before it. The first was the religious, spanning the two centuries of the Crusades (1100–1330 c.e.). The second was the economic, beginning with the fourteenth century c.e. and persisting up until 1800. The third and last phase was the psychological, heralding the introduction of political anti-Semitism, a product of the modern age.

The religious phase of persecution was the least dangerous of the three, but the most intriguing. The two most interesting examples are the ritual murder charges and the host-desecration accusations.

England has the honor of originating the ritual murder myth, but Germany holds the record for the largest number of such charges. This myth is based on the belief that during Passover the Jews killed a Christian child to use its blood to sprinkle over the Passover matzah. The fact that the Torah forbids Jews to eat or drink blood in any shape or form was not allowed to interfere with this cherished belief.

After two centuries, and after this superstition had reached epidemic proportions and hundreds of Jews had lost their lives, even popes and emperors became embarrassed. With a few judicious excommunications and hangings, this vogue was stopped.

The host-desecration charge was even more fascinating. "Host" comes from a Latin word meaning victim. It is the name for the round wafer of unleavened bread used in the Christian ceremony of Mass. The doctrine of transubstantiation holds that the wine drunk and the wafer eaten at Mass, becomes the blood and flesh of Jesus. The host-desecration charge was based on the belief that the Jews stole these wafers (the host) from churches and pierced them with a sharp instrument to make them bleed in a reenactment of the suffering of Jesus on the cross.

The most popular remedy for the crime of desecrating the host was burning a synagogue, preferably with some Jews in it. This fashion, too, came to an end with a few bans and hangings ordered by pope and emperor. They, too, thought it absurd that a wafer could be made to bleed.

There was another persecution of note during this period. This time it is not an individual but a book. This persecution centered around the burning of the Talmud. Such burning took place first in France in 1244 C.E., and thereafter sporadically in scattered European countries. The most interesting aspect of this phenomenon was that the Old Testament, the Torah, though occasionally burned by mobs during riots against the Jews, was never burned officially on orders by the church. The church viewed the Torah itself with respect, as the word of God. With the lone exception of Poland, where the Talmud was burned as late as the sixteenth century, that fashion had ended in Western Europe two centuries earlier.

Though the centuries from 100 to 1300 C.E. were agonizing ones for the Jews, this agony was not reserved for Jews only. Though the exotic titles of "ritual murder" and "host-desecration" were reserved for Jews, there were equally fanciful and equally illogical charges such as "witchcraft" and "heresy" applied to Christians. Though the labels were different, the result—painful death by burning, quartering, or flaying—was the same. Even as Jews were burned or hanged for host-desecration and ritual murder in one marketplace, Christians were burned or hanged in adjacent marketplaces for witchcraft and heresy.

These were some of the challenges facing the Jews in their First Adventure in Christian Europe. How could they respond to them?

23

The Decision-Makers

With the dawn of the tenth century C.E., history was about to place the scepter of Jewish destiny into the hands of the obscure Jews of Europe, who so far had achieved nothing of any significance. What would they do with this three-thousand-year-old Jewish cultural heritage? Would it disintegrate in their inept hands and undistinguished minds, or would these European Jews acquire the ability to carry on the Jewish heritage?

The Jews of Christian Europe were vaguely aware of Mishna and Gemara; they had in fact carried on some Responsa with the Geonim in the Islamic empire. The Mishna, written in beautiful Hebrew, they could understand. But the Gemara was written in Aramaic, incomprehensible to them.

However, some of the problems facing the Jews in Europe could not be solved by Talmud. Polygamy, for instance. Though Christian law forbade it, the Torah permitted it. That, and other problems, had to be met head on, the sooner the better. The question was, could the Talmud be made to yield a few more survival miles, or had the time come to abandon it?

The decision was made to have it both ways—first to solve the most immediate problem without the aid of the Talmud, and then to catch up later with the longer-range problems after taking a further look into the Talmud.

We have seen how in the past the Jews when confronted with new challenges sought new experts to help them. So, for instance, they had exchanged the Tannaim for the Amoraim, whom in turn they had exchanged for the Geonim. Now the Jews of Christian Europe did the same. They exchanged the Geonim back there in the Babylonian hinterland for a new team of experts, the Poskim, the decision-makers.

The Poskim did not create new law. They merely reintroduced old

99

ones. They were so skillful at this that one European Talmudist exclaimed, "From France will come the Torah, and the Word of God from Germany."

The first and most daring of the decision-makers, Gershom ben Judah (960–1028 C.E.), was born in Metz, but lived in Mainz where he headed a small yeshiva. Rumor had it that his son had been converted, some said forcibly, to Christianity and died before he could repent.

Gershom grandly convoked a synod in Mainz in the year 1000 C.E. For this decision, and the brilliant way in which he handled it, Jewish history has bestowed upon him the title of Light of the Exile.

At this synod, Gershom came up with an idea which in a gracious way sidestepped the Torah and Talmud without invalidating either. He suggested that the community pass a series of Takkanot, ordinances, which would not nullify anything in the Torah or Talmud but merely set some aspects aside for a specified number of years. So, for instance, it was agreed that polygamy, which is permitted but not demanded by the Torah, should be given up voluntarily for one thousand years. With time this ordinance became binding on all Jews in Europe. But, sometime after the year 2000 C.E., the problem of polygamy would again come up and a new synod would have to be convoked with a new vote taken on that question.

Another ordinance declared that no Jew could divorce his wife without her consent, except in cases of insanity and immoral behavior. This was a farsighted decree for those days when men could set aside their wives almost at will—except of course in Catholic Europe, where a divorce was practically impossible to get.

Several other remarkable takkanot were also passed. Eight centuries before it became part of the United States Constitution, the synod at Mainz forbade the opening of anyone's private mail without permission from the person to whom it was addressed.

The synod also changed the Roman idea of *caveat emptor*, that is, "let the buyer beware," to *caveat vendor*, "let the seller beware." It prohibited a seller from describing goods in a deceptive manner, or packaging goods in deceptive containers. These concepts did not find their way into Western law until our own day, when laws in the United States were finally passed to curb merchants deceiving the public with false packaging and labelling.

Gershom also wrote the world's first copyright law. The Torah forbids the removal of a neighbor's landmark (Deuteronomy 19:14); that is, it is a crime to remove fencing from a neighbor's property in order to claim it as one's own. From this passage in the Torah, Gershom deduced that an author's mind was also his private property, and that no one could steal another person's ideas. This Jewish concept of ideas as private property was not adopted by Western civilization until 1709 in England. Today, many nations still do not have copyright laws.

Since that first synod, Diaspora Jews have convoked synods in other places to solve other thorny problems. So, for instance, a synod convoked in 1250 C.E., forbade rabbis to excommunicate any Jew without the consent of the community.

Nevertheless, in spite of the success of these ordinances, many felt a Europeanized Talmud was greatly needed. History thoughtfully provided the right scholar for the job, Rashi (an acronym for his real name, Rabbi Shlomo Itzhaki, born in Troyes, France (1040–1105 C.E.). His task was so vital that it was said, "If not for Rashi, the Talmud would have been forgotten in all Israel," meaning among all Jews.

Rashi was an undistinguished yeshiva student. After graduation he joined his father's vineyard business. He later opened a small yeshiva where he began explaining the Talmud in Hebrew and French. His yeshiva became an instant success as students from all over Europe flocked to Troyes, a town of ten thousand French and one hundred Jews. Rashi found lodgings for his students among the Christians who loved this learned rabbi who taught the local priests Hebrew and translated French lullabies into the language of the Prophets.

In his yeshiva, Rashi put a European head on the shoulders of the Babylonian Talmud by writing a commentary on it. This he did with great literary skill, in beautiful fluent Hebrew, and with elegant French expressions which he used whenever Hebrew lacked the precise word. Because he employed over three thousand medieval French words and phrases, his writings have also become a source of study of medieval French. Rashi's commentary on the Talmud has become a Jewish heritage.

Rashi was not a Talmudist in the original sense; that is, he did not create the law. He was, however, a brilliant interpreter of Talmudic law, deciding what was best for the Jews of Europe. With him the First Adventure of the Jews in Christian lands came to an end. After him, the school of Poskim also began to decline in importance.

The Second Adventure

(1100–1500 C.E.)

The Jews—after surviving the zeal of crusading
Christians; after resisting the temptations of the
Renaissance; and after having fortified their
Judaism with the writings of a quartet of great
Talmudists—are herded into deadly ghettos with the
coming of the Reformation.

*Synagogue architecture usually reflected the prevailing
trends of the period and country in which the Jews
resided. The Altenschule in Prague, built in 1620,
unmistakably shows the Gothic influence.*

24

The Crusades, the Renaissance, and the Reformation

By the twelfth century C.E., a dark age had settled over the European continent. But, whereas the Christians lived in a world of universal ignorance and poverty, the Jews lived in enclaves of relative learning and prosperity. The Jews wished to preserve this status quo; the Christians hoped for change. History heeded the preference of the Christians.

Six centuries after the screw which held the Roman empire together had fallen out, the screw which held the feudal system together, also fell out. The primary causes for this failure were serfs who became dissatisfied with being serfs, nobles who became bored with the life of the feudal aristocracy, and a church that became fearful that its powers were being threatened. The church came up with a solution that had nothing to do with the Jews but had a devastating effect upon them.

Though Palestine had been in Arab hands since 638 C.E., it had never occurred to anyone that Rome and Jerusalem should be united in one holy political embrace. When that idea finally did occur to someone it was the Jewish mind of Pope Gregory VII (1073–1083 C.E.). It was a well kept Vatican secret that Pope Gregory VII was descended from an Italian Jew named Baruch, founder of the banking house of Pierlone in Rome, who in 1030 C.E. converted to Christianity. It is ironic to contemplate that had Pope Gregory VII lived in 1942, he would have been exterminated in a German concentration camp.

Gregory VII (known as Holy Satan to his friends), sold the idea of uniting Rome and Jerusalem to his successor, Pope Urban II, who envisioned one Crusade sufficient for the task. Instead he begot nine Crusades, the Renaissance, and the Reformation. The Crusades shattered feudalism; the Renaissance set men's minds free; and the Reformation ended the religious monopoly of the Vatican. Had Pope Urban known the consequences, he would never have given that speech in Cleremont in 1095 C.E. that set the whole thing in motion.

The Crusaders did not set out to kill Jews; they set out to kill Arabs. Yet they ended up killing more Christians than Arabs and Jews combined. The Jews were the incidental victims. A few samples from the annals of the Crusades will explain this paradox.

The first Crusade was launched in 1096 C.E., in two segments from French soil. The first segment, known as the People's Crusade, was an unruly mob of three-hundred thousand French from the lowest classes. By the time this motley crew had reached the Rhine, it had run out of provisions and began plundering and killing the Jews in its path. Some bishops did their best to stop the carnage, but to little avail.

The path to Palestine ran through Hungary. But long before the People's Crusaders reached that country, they also ran out of Jews. They now plundered and killed Christians, leaving a trail of smoldering Christian villages instead of Jewish ones.

The Hungarians and Bulgarians, reluctant to become the next victims, armed themselves, and massacred two-hundred thousand of the Crusaders. When the remnants reached Constantinople, the Greek Orthodox Christians who hated the Roman Catholics, led them into a trap of waiting Turks who massacred the rest of the Crusaders, using prisoners for archery practice.

The second segment, known as the Crusade of Princes, fared not much better. After a three-year march to Jerusalem, there were but twenty-five thousand Crusaders of the original six-hundred thousand. The rest had died of hunger or disease, or had been slaughtered by other Christians who feared the Crusaders more than they feared the Arabs.

Other Crusades followed. The fourth Crusade achieved the impossible—exceeding the first in brutality. Over one million Greek Catholics were slaughtered by the Roman Catholic Crusaders after Constantinople fell into their hands. It was a blessing that the Jews had been expelled from the Byzantine empire a few years previously, thus escaping the horrors that were meted out to the Christian population.

One might take comfort in the fact that Jews were not the only ones driven to the slaughterbench; Christians shared the same fate. The grandeur of Jewish history, however, does not lie in calamities and suffering, but in overcoming them, in having the ability to bounce back from adversity into the midst of future history.

The Crusades and their calamities are not important to Jewish or Christian history, but what followed is important. In the wake of the Crusades, Jews and Christians mingled in the new marketplaces of ideas. This mingling gave birth to the glorious period of the Renaissance, which led to the Reformation. The Reformation, in turn, helped shatter the feudal world, introduced capitalism, launched Protestantism—and shoved the Jews into ghettos.

Here is what happened. Christians, having gone off to the Crusades with supreme confidence in their own cultural superiority, came back badly shaken after beholding the splendor of the Arabs. The serfs no longer wanted to go back to the feudal farms which they now viewed as prisons. They settled in towns, swelling them into cities. Here they became artisans, merchants, and businessmen. A spirit of restlessness swept Europe. A reawakening of learning, known today as the Renaissance, was upon the land.

The Renaissance was born in a small quadrangle in Italy with Milan, Naples, Venice, and Genoa as the four anchor cities. From here its influence was spread to the rest of Western Europe.

Remarkably enough, this was the quadrangle where Jews had been concentrated for the previous six centuries (700–1300 C.E.). This was the most logical place for the Renaissance to be born—an area where the intellectual soil had already been spaded by the Jews.

Nevertheless, it was not Jews but Christians who produced the Renaissance, with painters like da Vinci and Michelangelo, with sculptors like Bernini and Donatello, with writers like Petrarch and Dante—and with hundreds of other geniuses who created immortal works in paint, stone, and words.

It is also the sad duty of the Jewish historian to relate that no Jew made the front ranks in the Renaissance hall of fame. In fact, the Jews failed to place anyone even in second or third rank. However, during the Renaissance, even fourth rank was good enough.

For the Jews, the two Renaissance centuries in Italy were a recapitulation of the good old Hellenistic days. There was practically no profession or job in which Jews were not represented. They were physicians, poets, astronomers, finance ministers, silversmiths, exporters, importers, scientific instrument makers. They were also shoemakers, sailors, tailors, peddlers, and jugglers. And, they were professional actors, dancers, composers—fourth-raters to be sure, but nevertheless among the first in Jewish history to enter the professions. Many also amassed great wealth. They became patrons of art, and engaged famed architects to design their homes and synagogues.

But, as in any paradise, there were also snakes in the Renaissance garden. As Christians flocked from the farms to the cities, they began to compete for the positions occupied by the Jews. They legislated the Jews out of their posts and went into business for themselves, especially in the field of moneylending. When the Jews had been moneylenders, the Christians had contemptuously referred to that profession as usury. Now that they were moneylenders themselves, they called it banking to make it sound more respectable.

The church, which opposed banking as un-Christian, denounced the Christian bankers as usurers, just as it had denounced the Jews. But to little avail. Christian bankers would rather go to hell rich than to heaven poor.

The Christians took over Jewish ideas about commerce with enthusiasm. They absorbed Jewish (and Arab) concepts about doing business with notes, checks, and bills of exchange instead of gold on the barrelhead. By the sixteenth century C.E., the takeover had been completed. The Jews were no longer needed to fuel the Christian economy. Slowly they were being driven out of one profession after another to eliminate them as competitors. Within another century the Jews would be reduced to peddling and petty moneylending.

But there were also danger signals for the Christian establishment. People no longer blindly believed in everything the church taught. Religious sects, whose members no longer believed in all Catholic dogmas, began to mushroom in Europe. The voice of heresy—that is, the voice of religious opposition—was now heard on the continent.

Amazingly enough, most of these Christian heretic sects contained some Jewish ideas. Like the Jews, some of these heretic sects did not believe in the virgin birth; others were against the worship of images. Like the Jews, some sects believed in the Jewish Sabbath, not Sunday, as a day of rest; and many of these sects regarded the laws of Moses as still valid.

Because so many of these heretic sects were concentrated mostly in areas where Jews were concentrated—southern France, western Germany, and northern Italy—the church began to associate heresy with Jewish influences. It viewed the Christian heretics as Judaizers, as people who spread the religion of the Jews among Christians.

As long as the heretic sects remained small, the church was tolerant. But as the voices of heresy grew louder, the church became alarmed. At first the church thought that burning a few heretic leaders might be a good cure. In Bohemia, for instance, John Huss, was burned alive (1415 C.E.). When this simple remedy did not help, Girolamo Savonarola in Italy received a triple sentence of torture, hanging, and burning (1498 C.E.).

But torture, hanging, and burning in all their combinations did not prove effective cures for heresy. The voice of the German monk Martin Luther (1483–1546 C.E.) drowned out all voices of moderation. He, more than anyone else, united most protesting sects into one religious reformation, and Protestantism was born.

The church now began to have second thoughts about its patience with the Jews. Perhaps the time had come not to wait another thousand years for their voluntary conversion to Christianity. Perhaps the time had come to isolate the Jews from the rest of the Christian population to prevent them from infecting Christian minds with ideas of religious freedom.

History came to the aid of the Church. A series of expulsions of Jews from West European states was making thousands upon thousands of Jews stateless, homeless, and rootless. No longer having rights as citizens, the Jews could be disposed of as displaced persons.

It is against this historical background that the Second Adventure of the Jews in Europe unfolds.

25

Jews, Marranos, and Limpieza de Sangre

The end of the Crusades heralded a new trend in Jewish history. Whereas from 600 to 1200 C.E. the Jews had been invited to settle in the countries of Western Europe, these same countries began expelling the Jews after 1200. The motivating spirit was greed.

England was the first. Christian scholars blame that expulsion on the usury of the Jewish moneylenders. But the record points to the chicanery of King Edward I (1272–1307 C.E.) who had a genius for larceny. First he stole ten thousand pounds sterling from the Templars*; then that organization was banned from England. Using the same tactic, he taxed the ten thousand Jews of England so heavily that it robbed them of all their money. He then expelled them in 1290 C.E. so he could appropriate their property and sell it for personal gain.

The people of England rejoiced; they thought they would not have to pay their debts to the Jews. But they did not fully appreciate their monarch. King Edward squeezed out of them every last penny they owed the Jews. Then he called in Italian usurers who went into partnership with the British clergy and aristocracy. This new Christian consortium of usurers raised interest rates so high that the Anglo-Saxons now mourned the departure of the Jews.

England was not only hypocritical in her stated reasons for expelling the Jews but also ungrateful. The Jews had contributed much to the evolving British common law, especially the jury system and the concept of due process of law.

When the Jews had arrived in England in the eleventh century C.E. at the invitation of William the Conqueror, they viewed the illiterate Anglo-

---

*A religious order of nobles, knights, and priests who had made vast fortunes fleecing the Crusaders.

Saxons with as much contempt as did the Norman conquerors. Accustomed as the Jews were to Talmudic concepts of judicial procedure based on evidence, they found the British custom of settling legal disputes through ordeal by fire and trial by combat especially barbaric.

The Jews informed the king they would not stay if, before they could collect a debt, they would have to first be burned to a crisp or sliced by a sword. They demanded that legal dispute be settled according to Jewish law. William, accustomed to settling disputes by flogging, hanging, or mass murder, nevertheless agreed with the Jews.

Talmudic law specifies that in cases of disputes about property, the verdict of a three-man court is binding. In England, the Jews worked out a compromise system—six Jews and six Christians acceptable to both sides in the dispute. After a century, even the Anglo-Saxons conceded that this was a better method than being slain in combat, and the jury system found its way into British common law.

Several of the main provisions of the Magna Carta (1215 C.E.) were concepts already embodied in the Torah or Talmud and introduced in England by the Jews. So, for instance, the due process of law provisions in the Magna Carta were first spelled out by Talmudists in the tenth century C.E. Maimonides stated it this way: "Every law which the king enacts for all . . . is not robbery. But when the king takes away from one person only, not in accordance with the law known to all . . . it is robbery."

The two main provisions of the due process of law—that men have the right to live by laws applicable to all, and that no crime can exist until there is a law forbidding that act to all—were embodied in Talmud commentaries for centuries before they were incorporated into the Magna Carta and later into the American Constitution.

Nevertheless, the Jews of England were expelled, and they showed bad judgment by fleeing to France. The French kings taxed all their money, confiscated their property, and also expelled them. The Jews were then permitted to return if they paid a fine for having left wonderful France in the first place.

This con game worked on and off for a century until the Jews finally got wise and stayed out of France. When there were no more Jews to fleece, the French kings began swindling the Templars. Which all goes to prove you don't have to be Jewish to get scammed, though it does help.

The French Jews fled to Germany, and here the game of expulsion and ransom reached new heights of cunning. As Germany at that time was nothing but a conglomerate of hundreds of small German states, the Jews were expelled and recalled by these states in an infinite variety of ways. But one could always count on the confiscation of property on one end and a stiff fine on the other.

These expulsions had been strictly revenue-raising ploys, usually cloaked in religious hypocrisy. Though disastrous to the individual Jew, the expulsions did not, however, endanger the main body of Jews in the rest of Europe.

But, with the expulsion of the Jews from Spain in 1492 C.E., the new ingredient of genuine religious bigotry was added to the spirit of greed. It was an explosive mixture which shattered the supremacy of the Spanish Jews, and shifted Jewish destiny from Western to Eastern Europe.

The shift in Jewish fortunes in Spain began in the middle of the thirteenth century C.E. By 1250, the *reconquistadores* had succeeded in driving out most of the Moors, and in reuniting most of Spain under the banner of Christ. The new Christian rulers invited the Jews to stay and help them in their task of rebuilding the country. The Jews, who regarded Spain as their homeland by virtue of having lived there for thirteen hundred years, stayed.

But, when the voices of heresy in the European continent began penetrating into Spain, the Spanish church became alarmed. The first victims of that alarm were not Jews but scientists. As early as 1305 C.E., Spain banned all science so effectively that to this date no major scientific discovery has been made by a Spaniard.

Next, Spain turned her attention to the Jews. The Spanish church was worried lest the Jews would become the same Judaizing influence in Spain as it was alleged they were in the rest of Europe. But, rather than expel the Jews at this time, Spain thought it her duty to convert them to Christianity instead.

Within one century Spain launched three major conversion drives—in 1319, 1350, and 1415. Statistically they were major victories for the church because the Jews converted in unprecedented numbers and with little resistance. Altogether, over a quarter-million out of a half-million Jews in Spain converted to Christianity, a phenomenon unique in Jewish history.

Cecil Roth summarizes this Christian success in his book *A History of the Marranos*: "In some places the Jews did not even wait for the application of compulsion to convert. They anticipated the popular attack by coming forward spontaneously, clamoring for admission to the church. All told, the number of conversions in the kingdoms of Aragon and Castile were reckoned at the improbable figure of two-hundred thousand."

Thus, after 1415 C.E., half the Jews in Spain were converts to Christianity. The Spanish Christians referred to them as conversos, the converted ones. The Jews, however, called them Marranos, a Spanish word meaning pigs or swine. But why in the world would the Jews refer to them as swine?

History has given us two portraits of the Marranos. The most popular one depicts them as pious Jews forcibly converted and forcibly kept in the Christian fold. Their love for Judaism was so great that at the risk of their lives they continued to practice Judaism in secret.

The more recent theory holds that, while some Marranos did practice Judaism in secret, many did not. They viewed themselves as the unaffiliated, believing neither in Talmud nor Gospels. The Jews, according to this view, saw the Marranos as godless apostates. The Christians saw them as heretics.

The Marrano problem began not with the first generation of baptized Jews, but with the second and third generations who, knowing little of Judaism, entered Christian society with enthusiasm. They rose to great positions of power and prestige, and married into the noblest families of Spain. Cecil Roth states that there was hardly an aristocratic family in Aragon that did not have Marrano blood in its veins. Even the church claimed Marrano bishops and archbishops.

The Christians, incensed at seeing their religion flaunted by these worldly Marranos, contemptuously referred to them as the new Christians. They were also galled by the fact that they, the old Christians, could not aspire to the lofty positions held by the Marranos.

In 1480 C.E., in Toledo, the old Christians raised a new, chilling cry of *limpieza de sangre*, purity of blood. They held that purity of blood, not ability, should determine who got the top positions in the realm. They claimed that only those Christians whose ancestry went back over a thousand years could have pure blood. This, of course, excluded the Marranos, whose Christianity went back only a century or less.

This cry of purity of blood had three immediate consequences. It led to the Inquisition. It led to the horrors of the auto-da-fé, an act of faith. And finally it led to the expulsion of the Jews from Spain in 1492 C.E. The act of faith was a euphemism for being burned alive.

The long-range consequences of this cry for *limpieza de sangre* were even more catastrophic. Four centuries later it became the slogan of racists, leading to the deaths of six million Jews in concentration camps.

The Inquisition, from a Latin word for "to inquire," was instituted in Spain in 1482 C.E., with Tomas Torquemada as the grand inquisitor. Its purpose was to inquire into the religious purity of those suspected of heresy.

Torquemada was not a callous twentieth-century-type racist bent on exterminating the Jews according to some final solution. If such had been the case, he could easily have had every Jew in Spain slain, for the Jews were a small, unarmed, totally helpless minority. He was an ordinary, garden variety bigot, concerned with stamping out heresy in Spain.

Those who were brought before the Inquisition were not converted Jews but Marranos and Christians suspected of heresy. Though some Jews were killed during those horrifying years, they were victims of mob rule, not of the Inquisition.

Of those found guilty of heresy, only a small segment were burned at these autos-da-fé. The actual horror was the Inquisition itself, with its tortures of the accused before a verdict was rendered.

Modern man views with horror the medieval practice of burning people for religious beliefs, yet sees nothing incongruous in shooting people for their political views. Yet fewer people were put to death in the past fifteen hundred years for religious reasons than have been put to death in fifty years by communist Russia and Nazi Germany alone for political reasons.

In 1492, the Jews of Spain were presented with an ultimatum—to convert to Christianity or be expelled. Of the estimated quarter of a million Jews left in Spain, fifty thousand chose conversion. The rest chose expulsion.

The expelled Spanish Jews fled mainly to Portugal, North Africa, and the Ottoman empire. Those who fled to Portugal became refugees again within a decade when Portugal followed Spain's example. This time, the Spanish and Portuguese Jews fled mainly to France, Amsterdam, and South America. Those who fled to Amsterdam, laid the foundation for the first Reform Judaism. A segment of those who fled to South America were funneled by history to North America where they became the first Jewish pioneers in the future United States.

Expulsion, as a problem solver, was to have universal application in future history. In the seventeenth century C.E., King Louis XIV of France expelled the Huguenots for religious reasons in the same way the Spanish and Portuguese had expelled the Jews. The modern age added massacres to expulsions. In this century we have had the massacre of the Armenians by the Turks; the massacre of the Ukrainians by the Russian communists; the massacre of the Jews by the German Nazis; and the massacre of the Cambodians by the Vietnamese communists.

The expulsion of the Jews from Spain constituted another watershed in Jewish history. By 1500 C.E., the goodwill of the Renaissance was over. In 1516, Venice held a formal opening for the first ghetto in Europe. From the viewpoint of the church it was none too soon. One year later, in 1517, Luther threw the gauntlet in the face of the Vatican by nailing his ninety-five theses to the door of the church in Wittenberg. Europe exploded in a series of religious wars for a century.

Luther, sincerely convinced that his Protestantism was a revived form of Judaism, made a bid for Jewish acceptance by beseeching the Jews to return to his "authentic" Judaism. When the Jews refused, he turned bitterly against them.

Until his rejection by the Jews, Luther's writings on the Jews sounded like the blurbs by a public relations director: "The Jews are blood relations of our Lord," Luther wrote. "If it were proper to boast of flesh and blood, the Jews belong more to Christ than we . . . We must receive them kindly and allow them to compete with us in earning a livelihood."

But, after the Jews refused to become Protestants, it was another story. Then he wrote: "First their synagogues should be set fire, and whatever does not burn should be covered with dirt . . . and this ought to be done for the honor of God and Christianity so that God may see we are Christians."

Luther's fury, however, was not directed just at Jews; he turned against anyone who opposed him—Jews, popes, kings and peasants—denouncing them all in his magnificently malevolent prose.

The sixteenth century heralded the shift from the Middle Ages to the modern age. With the success of the Reformation, the power of the Catholic church was broken, and the pendulum of history swung from faith to reason. But reason was not the liberator people had been promised, especially not for the Jews. Values were no longer determined by the church but in the marketplace. The Jews were no longer viewed as a living testament to Jesus, and thus no longer needed to be protected. Jews became the superfluous ones on the continent.

In assessing the role of the church in Jewish history from 500 to 1500 C.E., it is clear that the church had certainly not been a friend of the Jews. But neither had it been a deadly enemy. The church was against Judaism, not the Jews. The moment a Jew converted to Christianity, he became an honored member of the Christian community. Though the church's role in helping institute the ghetto was an ignominious one, this policy was not as inhuman as the final solutions devised by the modern totalitarian states of right and left. Anti-Semitism as a calculated policy to remove the Jews from the midst of society by wholesale murder was a policy of the modern age, not that of the church. Fewer Jews were killed on the entire continent of Europe from 500 to 1500, when the church was in power, than were killed in the twelve years when Hitler was in power.

We have explored the outer Christian wrappings of the Second Adventure, but what about the inner, Jewish core? How fared Judaism itself during these four incredible Crusades-Renaissance centuries?

26

The Prepared Table

The challenge of the Crusades has been dangerous but not complicated. The solution was not in a new Talmud but in getting out of the path of the Crusaders to avoid being killed. Essentially it was a good remedy, for the next eight Crusades were not as devastating to the Jews as was the first.

Because Jewish life during the two centuries of the Crusades was much the same as in the two preceding ones, Gershom's prescription (for minor religious headaches, take Takkanot) and Rashi's remedy (when in doubt consult your nearest decision-maker) were in the main still valid.

However, for new acute problems, Rashi's children and grandchildren patented a new, improved strain of Rashi's remedy. They called it Tosafot, from the Hebrew meaning "to add." In modern terminology it probably would be called booster shots. And of course, the practitioners of Tosafot were called Tosafists.

But, as the Tosafists multiplied, their remedies also multiplied. As one Talmudic, scholar, Jacob ben Asher, was to express the problem—"Their reasoning became faulty, controversy increased, and opinions multiplied." Chaos was the result.

Nevertheless, for almost two centuries the Tosafists dominated the religious scene until three things happened: Rashi ran out of brilliant descendants; a clash broke out between the Jews in Spain and the Jews in Western Europe; and the Renaissance made its debut.

A new Jewish social problem was emerging in Europe. Through the course of five centuries (600–1100 c.e.), two Judaisms had developed independently of each other. One was Sephardi, or Spanish Judaism; the other was Ashkenazi, or German Judaism. When they finally clashed in the twelfth century, their customs differed so much that not only did they look upon each other with contempt, but they went so far as to use different prayerbooks and refuse to eat each other's food. Each accused the other of not being kosher.

The Shephardi culture expressed itself in Arabic, Spanish, and Hebrew, and developed a new folk-language, Ladino, based on Spanish mixed with Hebrew. Though Ladino has produced no literature, it has nevertheless persisted to this day.

115

The Ashkenazi culture expressed itself in German and Hebrew. It, too, developed a folk-language, Yiddish, with a base in German and also mixed with Hebrew. In the nineteenth century, Yiddish suddenly became a medium for a magnificent literature, now the heritage of mankind. But, in the twentieth century, when so many Jews died in Nazi concentration camps, Yiddish all but disappeared as a language.

The Renaissance engulfed the Ashkenazi Jews at about the same time the Sephardi Jews began breaking out of Spain. This put an end to the Tosafists who were no match for the sophisticated Spanish Talmudists. The time had come for the Ashkenazi to produce their own Talmudic scholars or become engulfed by the Shephardi culture.

God's wishes happily coincided with the needs of the Ashkenazim. After languishing for three centuries (1000–1300 C.E.), behind the Spanish Jews in Talmudics, the Ashkenazi Jews suddenly broke out of their hibernation and produced a dazzling series of Talmudic scholars.

Three of the many stand out, because they detected coming trouble rather than merely diagnosing existing ills. The first, Jacob ben Asher (1270–1340 C.E.), a German Talmudist, unified all Talmudic currents— Arabic, Spanish, French, German—into one Jewish mainstream. The second, Joseph Caro (1488–1575), a Spanish polygamist, provided the Jews with a portable "smorgasbord" of law to preserve them in their coming three-century ghetto imprisonment. The third, Moses Isserles (1530–1572) a millionaire Polish dillettante astronomer and renowned Talmudist, threw an Ashkenazi "tablecloth" over Caro's Sephardi "table."

The task of healing the rift between the Spanish Talmudists and the French Tosafists fell on the shoulders of German-born Jacob ben Asher, poor as a yeshiva mouse. Educated in Germany on the French Tosafists, he moved to Toledo, Spain, where he studied the Spanish Talmudists.

Toward the end of his life, Jacob ben Asher published the results of a lifetime of work, a volume entitled *The Four Rows*, a code of Talmudic law rivalling that of Maimonides. In it he brought together three centuries of Jewish life and thought in Spain, France, and Germany, so brilliantly that the Sephardim forgave him for eating the effete foods of France, and the Ashkenazim overlooked his penchant for the strange oriental foods of Spain. The code also had its desired effect. *The Four Rows* began the unification of the Jews of Europe into one Judaism.

If Joseph Caro had not existed, it would be impossible to invent him, for he is one of Judaism's most improbable figures. He was married five times—to this fifth wife at the age of seventy-nine—and it seems that he was also married to more than one wife at the same time. In his diary, Caro wrote he wanted to be a martyr, and that his highest wish was to be burned at the stake for the greater glory of God. Wisely, he stayed out of Christian Europe where his wish might have been fulfilled.

Caro also records in his diary his conversations with a maggid, a messenger of God, who styled himself as "the son of Mishna." This maggid, Caro wrote, came to visit him at night, whispering in his mouth endearments like "Lo, I am the Mishna speaking in your mouth, kissing you with kisses of love." The maggid also revealed to a stunned Caro that his third wife, in a previous stage of transmigration, had been a famed rabbinic scholar.

Caro may have been an eccentric in his private life, but that did not prevent him from becoming a Talmudic genius. His encyclopedic knowledge of Jewish law and his clarity of expression elevated his Talmud code into a great classic in Judaism.

Joseph Caro was born in Toledo, Spain. In 1492, when he was four years old, his family chose expulsion rather than conversion to Christianity. Eventually Caro settled in Safed, Palestine, then part of the Ottoman empire. Here he founded a small yeshiva; here he wrote his famed code, *The Prepared Table*, first published in 1565.

We do not know what motivated Caro to call his work *The Prepared Table*, but that is what it was, figuratively and literally. In this slim volume, Caro compressed fifteen-hundred years of Mishna, Gemara, commentaries, footnotes, amendments, amplifications, and closings. Here on display were the edifices of Hanasi, Arrika, Samuel, Ashi, Maimonides, Asher, all neatly prepared, easily digested. It was a smorgasbord of Jewish law, tailored for Jews living in isolated ghettos, where every Jew could help himself to the right law, for the right purpose, at the right time.

However, even perfection has flaws. The adulation for Caro's work did not come instantly. Because *The Prepared Table* was laden with Sephardi traditions, the Ashkenazi Jews, who had become the dominant majority, refused to sit down at that Spanish table.

But even the most anti-Sephardi scholars recognized the brilliance of Caro's work; it was just a question of how to make it kosher for the Ashkenazim. To their rescue came another one of those improbable members of Jewish history. This time it was Moses Isserles, an Orthodox Jewish Aristotelian philosopher from Cracow, Poland, known as "the Maimonides of the Polish Jews."

To make Caro's work relevant to Ashkenazi life, Isserles wrote a companion piece to *The Prepared Table* calling it, perhaps tongue in cheek, *The Tablecloth*. Henceforth, this Sephardi table and Ashkenazi tablecloth went together like a bride and groom. It is this combined work which is now generally referred to as the *Shulchan Aruch,* the Hebrew name for prepared table.

Did Caro write this commentary with the future needs of the ghetto in mind? It is anyone's guess, but the timing was perfect. The gates to the first ghetto had been opened in 1516; fifty years later ghettos were mushrooming all over Europe. It was at this point, in 1565, that *The Prepared Table* was published, destined to become the chief instrument for Jewish spiritual survival for three centuries.

With this first ghetto in Venice, the Third Jewish Adventure in Christian Europe began.

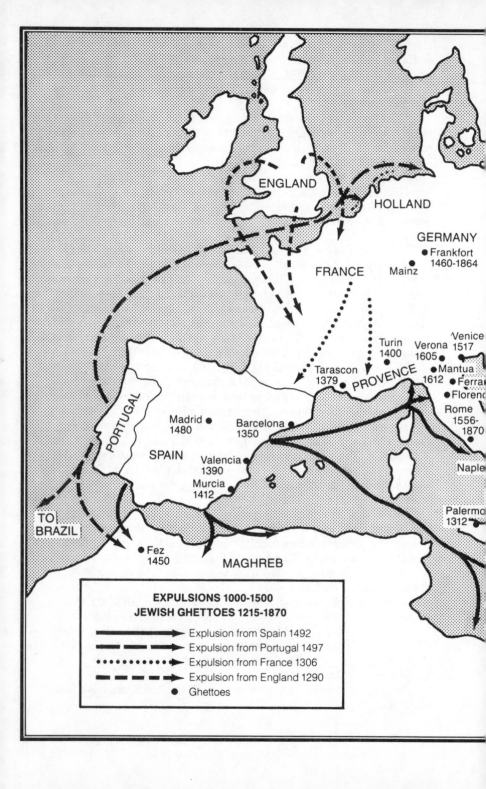

EXPULSIONS 1000-1500
JEWISH GHETTOES 1215-1870

⟶ Explusion from Spain 1492
⟶ Explusion from Portugal 1497
⟶ Explusion from France 1306
⟶ Explusion from England 1290
● Ghettoes

ENGLAND

HOLLAND

GERMANY
● Frankfort
1460-1864
Mainz

FRANCE

Venice
1517
Turin   Verona
1400   1605
Tarascon   Mantua
1379   PROVENCE   1612   Ferra
                              Florenc
Madrid ●   Barcelona ●   Rome
1480   1556-
PORTUGAL   1870
SPAIN
        Valencia
        1390   Naple
        Murcia
        1412
TO   Palermo
BRAZIL   1312
        ● Fez
        1450   MAGHREB

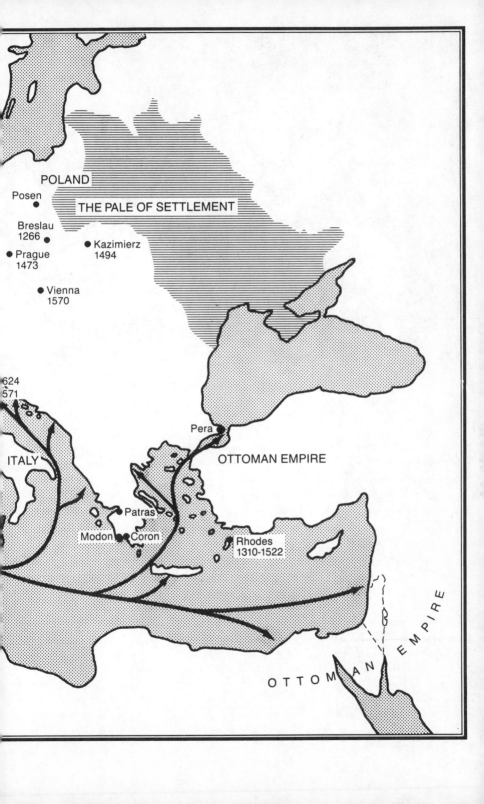

NAPOLÉON LE GRAND,

rétablit le culte des Israélites, le 30 Mai 1806.

Une antique nation, autrefois l'unique dépositaire des volontés du Trèshaut, et gouvernée par la divine législation de Moïse, est dispersée depuis plus de dix-sept Siècles sur la surface du globe. En rapport avec tous les Peuples, elle ne se mêle avec aucun, et elle semble exister pour voir passer devant elle le torrent des siècles qui les entraîne. Un tel phénomène serait inexplicable, s'il ne tenait qu'à l'ordre politique, car il était moralement impossible que les Juifs pussent longtems exister, malgré toutes les vicissitudes et les persécutions dont ils furent les victimes chez les différentes nations de la terre. Dans combien de proscriptions ne furent-ils pas envellopés! Pour ne parler que de la France, qui ne sait les haines, les mépris, les outrages, les confiscations, les bannissemens, les supplices même qu'ils y ont endurés? rien de cruel, rien de deshonorant ne leur a été épargné; de sorte que l'on serait tenté de croire que nos aïeux ne les comptaient point au nombre des humains. En vain quelques orateurs éloquens s'élevèrent contre une si criante injustice, leur voix ne fut point entendue, et les infortunés Israélites paraissaient à jamais condamnés à l'avilissement et à l'opprobre. Un nouveau Cyrus a paru, mais il a fait pour eux plus que l'ancien. S'il n'a pas reconstruit leur temple, il leur a donné une patrie et des loix protectrices de leur culte et de leurs droits civils; en les rendant citoyens et membres de la grande nation, il leur a rendu l'honneur; en leur donnant des mœurs, il les a garantis pour jamais du mépris de ses peuples. Pénétrés de reconnaissance pour de si précieux bienfaits, les enfans d'Israël se sont prosternés au pied du trône du Grand Napoléon, et les filles de Sion ont fait retentir les voûtes des temples de ces cantiques célèbres que répétaient les échos du Jourdain, lorsqu'au retour de sa captivité le peuple Hébreu célébrait les miséricordes du Seigneur. La gratitude des Israélites français ne s'est pas bornée à de simples démonstrations, ils prouvent chaque jour qu'ils sont dignes des faveurs du Souverain par leur attachement à son auguste personne et par leur soumission à ses loix.

The Third Adventure

(1500–1800 C.E.)

The Jews—whose ideas until now have roamed the universe—are stripped of their liberties and confined to the cramped view of the world through ghetto windows, stage three self-destructive revolts against their fate, and are at last delivered from their hell by a Jewish hunchback and a French emperor.

For emancipator of the Jews from the ghettos of Europe, history chose no less a personage than Napoleon the Great who, styling himself another Cyrus, convoked a Great Sanhedrin to affirm that liberation.

27

The Nightmare

Had history played a cruel joke on the Jewish people? In this Third Adventure, it had flung this proud, inventive people into a dungheap known as the ghetto, there to live in squalor for three nightmarish centuries (1550–1850).

The term "ghetto" has been trivialized in the twentieth century to mean merely an ethnic neighborhood, like "black ghetto" or "Italian ghetto." But the medieval Jewish ghetto was a physical prison in which Jews were forcibly stored like an unneeded product awaiting future disposal.

The usual Jewish ghetto consisted of a main street with a synagogue at one end and a cemetery at the other, housing about 150 to 300 people, seldom over a thousand. It was usually enclosed by a wall with one gate serving as both entrance and exit. The gate was opened at sunup from the outside and closed at sundown—and woe unto anyone found outside after that hour.

The ghetto flourished in Central Europe, mainly in German-speaking lands. In East European countries, the majority of the Jews had been herded into small villages and towns known as shtetls, from the German word for city. The shtetl was not surrounded by physical walls like the ghetto, but by invisible barriers of restrictions.

The lofty vocations of Renaissance days had disappeared. Jews were now mainly tailors, butchers, wagonmakers. They were saloonkeepers, moneylenders, peddlers. Jewish education, which until the fourteenth century had run the gamut from Aristotelian logic to the natural sciences, now was restricted mainly to the study of Torah and Talmud.

The most hated aspect of ghetto life for the Jews was the special dress they were generally forced to wear to identify them as Jews. Though the clothing was often ludicrous, and always meant to demean, the Jews showed their defiance by wearing this garb with dignity.

To insulate themselves from the sneers and insults hurled at them by scabrous, besotted Jew-baiters, the Jews wrapped themselves in evermore layers of traditions. So effective was this protective cocoon of ritual swaddling that the Jews came to look upon their detractors as ignorant hooligans and upon themselves as respositories of virtue. Within a century that attitude of contempt was transferred to all Christians.

Though ghetto life itself was demeaning, family and communal life was dignified. High moral standards prevailed. Though robbery, rape, and murder of Gentiles by Gentiles were rampant outside ghetto walls, crimes of violence were practically nonexistent inside. One day each week, Sabbath candles blotted out the misery of ghetto life, fortifying the Jews for the coming week's assaults upon their dignity.

Both ghetto and shtetl were instituted to isolate the Jew so that his religion would not affect the Christians. However, the moment a Jew converted to Christianity, he no longer was abhorred; he became an honored Christian. Thus conversion to Christianity became for many Jews a "passport to civilization," as the German poet Henrich Heine, who took that route, called it.

Other Jews managed to slip out of the ghetto by virtue of their wit and genius, without converting. They became the famed "court Jews" and the glittering "salon Jews."

The crowned heads of Europe, having sensed the financial flair of the Jews, began recalling such Jews from the ghettos, entrusting into their hands the financial affairs of the state. They became the court Jews, with immense power. They created for the king the institutions that eventually became the financial foundations of the modern state.

Of the two hundred independent states of the Holy Roman Empire, as Germany was then known, almost every ruler had his court Jew. Even that most powerful Catholic fanatic, Emperor Charles V, had one—the famed Yossl of Rosheim, a Jew so powerful that the nobles feared him, yet so essential to the king that he could not dispense with him.

Perhaps the most colorful court Jew was Joseph Süss Oppenheimer, finance minister to the Duke of Wurttenburg. Süss's life resembles a flamboyant character in a Dumas novel more than that of a medieval Jew.

Süss (1698–1738) was the illegitimate son of a beautiful Jewish actress and the handsome Christian, Marshall von Heydersdorff of Wolfenbuttel—one of those mini-states that serve as background for Strauss operettas. As Jewish law holds that any child is Jewish as long as the mother is, Süss was a Jew. As Christian law held that no matter who the mother is, the child is Christian if the father is, S³uss was a Christian.

Unaware of his paternity, Süss grew up as a Jew, not in a ghetto, but among Christian aristocrats because his mother was a famed salon Jew. Throughout his career, he refused to convert to Christianity, using all his powers to help his hapless fellow Jews in the ghettos.

When the duke suddenly died, the nobles had Süss arrested and condemned to death. In prison, he learned of his father's identity. All he had to do was to reveal who he was and he would be set free to enjoy the life of royalty. But Süss, who had lived as a Jew and enjoyed the thrills of living by his wits, was not about to change roles now. Proud of being a Jew, he accepted his death sentence in silence.

As Süss walked with dignity to the gallows, the Christians pelted him with dung, while the Jews chanted the Sh'mah. That night Jews, risking their lives, cut down his body, clothed it in silks and buried him in a secret grave, intoning the Kaddish over the son of Marshall von Heydersdorff.

Quite different is the story of the salon Jew whose life was a cross between that of a Marrano and a court Jew. The salon Jews had used their native talents to escape the ghetto. They were mostly children of parents who had acquired great wealth in a variety of occupations such as banking and in the pioneering of new industries. Rich, talented, educated, these salon Jews became patrons of art, literature, music, theater. To their salons came Christian artists, writers, painters—men and women of talent. Members of high society and royalty, eager to meet these famous people, were drawn to the soirees of the salon Jews.

The life of court Jews and salon Jews was, however, only for the favored few upon whom fate had bestowed the necessary wit, talent, and beauty to make it. The vast majority of Jews languished in their ghetto prisons, praying for deliverance.

The ghetto period was the first regression in Jewish history. It was also to have a disastrous impact on the future image of the Jew. Before they were herded into the ghettos of Europe, the Jews were renaissance men of many talents. But after a three-century isolation in the ghetto, the Jew became a caricature of his former self, a symbol of derision. New generations of Christians who had not known the proud Jew of past years looked with scorn or pity on this degraded, dehumanized Jew—the only Jew they knew.

But the remarkable aspect of this phase in Jewish history is that in spite of it all, the Jews did not lose the inner vision of themselves as God's Chosen People. Always in touch with God through the Torah, the Jew was to come back into world history, again a man of valor, a man of grandeur.

28

Revolt in the Ghetto

After a hundred years of ghetto life, the Jews were just about ready to go out of their minds. For a people that had roamed the civilized world as freemen since the days of Joshua, this ignominious imprisonment was a demeaning slap at its soul. They wanted out, OUT, OUT!

But how? They had no weapons, no armies. Conversion to Christianity was a sure method of escape, but the Jews were not inclined to convert en masse as had the Marranos in Spain. And only few of the ghetto dwellers had the endowments to qualify as court or salon Jews.

Unable to stage a revolt against their Christian oppressors, the Jews staged three revolts against the Talmud instead.

After a century of ghetto life, doubts began to creep into the minds of many ghetto dwellers as to the ability of the Talmud to keep Judaism afloat. The ever increasing layers of tradition and ritual spun by the Talmudists were seen by many as a suffocating web. Two opposing views developed—one, that these rituals preserved Jewish life, the other that they constricted it. It was the tension between these two views that exploded in the three revolts against the Talmud.

Consternation befell the Talmudists when Leon de Modena (1571–1648), a Venice-born scholar whose father had been knighted by Emperor Charles V, published two books which embodied this dual view of the Talmud. In one book published under his own name, he brilliantly defended the Talmud, showing how it sustained Jewish life. In his second book, published anonymously, he launched an equally brilliant attack on the Talmud, pointing out its maiming effects on the Jewish spirit. Soon after this attack on the Talmud, came the first of the three revolts against it.

Jewish history, so rich in creating improbable characters, now outdid itself. This time history sent the Jews two psychos and a Hasid. They were

126

a charlatan named Sabbatai Zvi (1626–1676) who, like a pied piper, led a third of the Jews down the road of apostasy; a sex maniac named Jacob Frank (1726–1791), who introduced licentiousness as a new dimension to Judaism; and a mystic called Baal Shem Tov (1700–1760), who sold the Jews on the idea that they could sing and dance themselves into God's grace.

The first of this trio, Sabbatai Zvi, born in Turkey, was a psycho who heard voices telling him he was the messiah. In a public ceremony, he had himself married to the Torah, declared himself the messiah, and abolished the Talmud. The stunned rabbis promptly excommunicated him, but to no avail. A third of Europe's Jews, searching for the long-awaited salvation, flocked to Sabbatai's messianic tents.

Then Sabbatai overreached himself. He gathered an army, and announced he was going to depose the sultan of the Ottoman empire and restore Palestine as a homeland for the Jews. The sultan clapped the madman in jail, and gave him the usual choice that winners give to losers—conversion or death. Sabbatai chose conversion, and his influence came to an end.

But the spirit of the Sabbatean revolt did not die. Embers of the rebellion smoldered, and within a century there were two new revolts, Frankism and Hasidism.

Jacob Frank, founder of Frankism, born in the Ukraine, became a travelling salesman in Turkey. He proclaimed himself a prophet, but his followers elevated him to full messiahship. Under his leadership, Frankism was a heresy dedicated to the cult of sex.

Like Sabbatai, Frank abolished the Talmud. As with Sabbatai, the rabbis excommunicated him, but, again, to little avail. Ghetto Jews flocked to Frank's banners, seeking an outlet for their misery.

History repeated itself. Frank converted, not to Islam but to Christianity, asking his followers to do likewise. Most Jews declined but those who did were welcomed with open arms by the Polish aristocracy. And thus the riffraff of Jewish society was assimilated into Polish nobility.

Almost contemporaneously with Frankism, spread yet a third revolt, becoming more Jewish than Talmudism itself. It was a passive revolt of the followers of Israel ben Eliezer who transformed the sexual frenzy of the Frankists into the religious frenzy of the Hasidim, from the Hebrew word for "piety."

Israel ben Eliezer, known as the Baal Shem Tov, master of the good name, was also born in the Ukraine, of poor and ignorant parents. Two traditions have been handed down about him—one that he was a lazy bum, a truant from the heder who could neither read nor write; the other that he only pretended to be stupid so that he could study in secret.

Baal Shem married a rich man's ugly, elderly daughter, but that did not help him financially. The father of the bride took one look at the nebbish his daughter was about to marry and disinherited her. The couple settled down to a life of poverty, but eventually Baal Shem became a tavernkeeper. At the age of forty, his disciples aver, he threw off his cloak of ignorance, ready at last to declare himself a saint.

In Baal Shem's view, all men were equal before God, except the ignorant who were a little more equal than the others. In his doctrines, his followers thought they had found the Jewish spirit without having to spend years studying the Talmud. In one fell swoop, Bal Shem turned weakness into strength, defeat into triumph. He gave the Jews the spiritual fuel for the mileage ahead.

Hasidism swept like an anachronistic bingo game through ghetto and shtetl. It was a rebellion against the values of the old order. Starved culturally and emotionally, the Jews found in Hasidism a mystical outlet for their pent-up frustrations. It seemed to make the present more tolerable.

After the death of the Baal Shem, Hasidism was shattered into hundreds of ineffectual sects quarreling with each other. By 1850, its influence had waned.

But all had not been in vain. The failure of Sabbateanism, Frankism, and Hasidism created a willingness among the Jews to accept reason rather than ritual as a problem solver. Was it not time now for God to send a modern liberator?

History in a moment of generosity sent not one but two liberators. But no one could have imagined a more odd pair of heroes who arrived to rescue the Jews—an ugly Jewish hunchback from the ghetto of Dessau, Germany, and a charismatic Christian conqueror, the emperor of France.

29

The Hunchback
and the Emperor

In 1743, a hunchbacked, fourteen-year-old boy, son of an impoverished Torah scribe in the ghetto of Dessau, stumbled upon two books forbidden to nice Jewish children. One was *A Guide to the Perplexed* by Maimonides; the other an essay by John Locke.

Before the boy read these two books, he believed all virtue resided in Jews and all evil in Christians. Jewish education in his day had shrunk to only the study of the Hebrew alphabet, Torah, and Talmud. All else was forbidden as trefah, unclean. Should a misguided youth forsake the ghetto and study medicine, law, engineering, or the sciences, the parents of that child would sit shiva; that is, mourn for him. In the mind of the fundamentalists, that child had crossed over and was considered dead.

The two books the young lad had discovered opened windows to his mind. The ghetto no longer could hold him. He escaped by simply walking out one morning when the ghetto gate opened, and not returning that evening when it closed.

After many adventures, our truant reached Berlin where he acquired an education in languages, philosophy, and science—all subjects forbidden him in the ghetto. He learned that great changes had taken place in the world in the two hundred years between 1550 and 1750.

While the Jews had languished in the ghettos, the Christians had conquered the world with their ideas. Galileo, Kepler, and Newton had reshaped man's thinking about heaven and earth. Bacon, Descartes, and Spinoza (who was an excommunicated Jew) had revolutionized philosophy. The Christians, in those two centuries, had viewed the paintings of Rembrandt and Goya, attended the plays of Shakespeare and Molière, listened to the music of Vivaldi and Bach. Conquistadores had added the American continents to the world, and daring adventurers had sailed around Africa to India and China.

This was the world the son of the Torah scribe set out to conquer with his mind. He became a master stylist of the German language, and the leading salon Jew in Berlin. Three of his five children converted to Christianity, and his grandson Felix, who became a world-renowned composer, was baptized at birth. And this leading salon Jew himself might have ended up at a baptismal font had not a Swiss theologian taunted him into either becoming an honest Jew or else converting to Christianity.

It was at this point that Moses Mendelssohn (1729–1788), the hunchback from Dessau, stopped running, appraised himself, and chose Judaism. He realized he had not been running away from Judaism but from the image of the Jew created by the ghetto. To him, the authentic Jew was not the ghetto Jew, but the historic Jew before the ghetto age.

Now Mendelssohn had but one thought in mind—how to help free the Jews from their mental and physical ghettos and restore the image of the authentic pre-ghetto Jews. The challenge essentially was the same as in Babylonian, Hellenistic, Islamic, and Renaissance days—how to fashion a Judaism that would permit the Jew to be both a Jew and world citizen at the same time.

Mendelssohn correctly appraised the world around him. The forces which had herded the Jews into ghettos in the sixteenth century had been defeated. Catholic Spain had been shattered with the sinking of her Armada by the British; France had introduced religious freedom with the Edict of Nantes; the power of the church had been broken with the Treaty of Westphalia. Jews had settled in the Netherlands, been readmitted to England, and they again resided in France. Perhaps the new forces of the Enlightenment sweeping Europe would also let the Jews out of the ghettos.

Mendelssohn clearly saw the dilemma of the ghetto Jews. On the one hand, if stuck forever in the ghettos like flies in amber, they would eventually die of cultural starvation. On the other hand, if suddenly liberated without preparation, the majority of young Jews would forsake their ghetto Judaism—the only Judaism they knew—in order to quickly make their passage to Western civilization.

Mendelssohn had a plan. Only Yiddish and Hebrew were taught in the ghettos. He decided to teach Jewish youth the German language, on the theory that once they knew that language, the knowledge of the world would be open to them.

But how could it be done? Very simply, said Moses Mendelssohn. He translated the Torah into German but used Hebrew letters, placing the Hebrew opposite of the German text. Now those who could read the Hebrew could read and understand the German. Understanding German, Jewish youth quickly taught themselves the Roman alphabet, and the world of ideas outside the ghetto walls was now open to them.

The ghetto no longer could hold its restless youth. More and more Jews squeezed out through the cracks in the walls into the world outside—a world now more tolerant to receive them, no longer demanding conversion to Christianity as the price. And waiting for them was Mendelssohn, with his new modern philosophy of Judaism.

Mendelssohn was the first Jew in history to advocate a separation of state and synagogue. He held that breaking a religious law was the concern of the individual only, not of state or synagogue. Each individual should be free to practice his Judaism and pursue any vocation as he saw fit, without fear of excommunication. He foresaw the time when self-governing ghettos would not be tolerated by any government. The Jews, he warned, would have to learn how to become citizens in the new modern state.

Was Moses Mendelssohn a liberator of the Jewish people or was he a prophet of deceit? History vindicated him. Shortly after his death, the French Revolution tore down the physical ghetto walls and set the Jews loose into the nineteenth century. And now Napoleon Bonaparte confronted the Jews with the questions Mendelssohn had posed.

There were about fifty thousand Jews in France at the time of the Revolution. Ten thousand were Sephardim, the intellectual and professional elite, mostly descendants of a segment of Jews who had been expelled from Spain in 1492.

The rest were Ashkenazim, most of them living in the province of Alsace-Lorraine, acquired by France in a war with Germany. They were the peddlers, the moneylenders, the petty shopkeepers. Both Sephardim and Christians looked upon them with contempt.

The French revolutionaries, who viewed the Sephardim as equals, granted them immediate citizenship. But it took two years of debates to convince the revolutionaries that the Ashkenazim, too, were entitled to such rights. France thus became the first country in Europe to grant all Jews full citizenship.

When Napoleon came to power, he wanted all Jews out of the ghettos, not out of any love for them, but because he wanted no enclave within the state which might become future trouble spots. Bluntly he told the Jews, "To the Jews as Frenchmen, everything; to the Jews as Jews, nothing."

Napoleon demanded that the French Jews openly declare their prime loyalty to the state and forswear any dual citizenship to the Talmud or any rabbi. To force such an open declaration, he summoned (in 1806) an assembly of Jewish notables to affirm Jewish ties to France as Frenchmen of the Mosaic faith.

The assembly affirmed all points. But to make them binding on all Jews in Napoleonic Europe, Napoleon played his trump card. He convoked a Sanhedrin, the first since the fall of Jerusalem in 70 C.E. The move stunned the Jews, but also moved them to tears of pride and hope.

The Sanhedrin affirmed that the Jews were not a governing minority within a state, that all Jewish laws in the Disaspora were only religious, and that French courts had precedence over Jewish courts except in religious matters.

These and other affirmations made by this Sanhedrin did not set any precedents in Jewish history. They were merely reaffirming the first Diaspora laws of survival hammered out by Jewish survival leaders beginning with Johanan ben Zakkai.

Napoleon's formula was used by every democratic state where the ghettos were abolished. The Jews now ceased to be a nation within a nation. Instead they became Jewish citizens among non-Jewish citizens, a religion among other religions.

But, whereas King Cyrus of Persia back in 500 B.C.E. received several paragraphs of praise in the Old Testament for liberating the Jews from Babylonian exile, Napoleon got mixed reviews in the Jewish press for emancipating the Jews from the ghetto. The liberals greeted his edict with joy, best expressed by the suave Sephardi financier who had served as president of Napoleon's Sanhedrin. "The function of this body," he said, "is to bring us back to the practice of our ancient virtues . . . to reawaken in the Jews a sense of their dignity by insuring them the enjoyment of their rights."

The fundamentalist Jews had another view, best summed up in the words of an anonymous rabbi in Poland. As the armies of Napoleon advanced, an excited student ran to this rabbi jubilantly shouting, "Rabbi, rabbi, the liberators are coming. At long last we shall be free and secure, treated like human beings, given dignity, and—"

But the rabbi interrupted him. "Yes, we shall be rich and safe," he said sadly, "And we will forget all about God, His law, His commandments, run after worthless goals. I'd rather be poor and oppressed as we are now, but faithful to our Judaism."

These two views—that of the Sephardi aristocrat and that of the Polish rabbi—were to become the crux of the dilemma that ensued as the Jews stepped from their sixteenth-century ghettos into the nineteenth-century world.

With the Third Adventure in Western civilization over, the Jews entered their Fourth Adventure. It was to be their most awesome and most magnificent, their most debasing and most ennobling, their most frightening and most promising.

The Fourth Adventure

(1800–2000 C.E.)

Sixteenth-century Jews, at last emancipated from their three-century long ghetto imprisonment, march into the nineteenth century, enlightenment where, within one generation, they become scientists, statesmen, and avant-garde intellectuals, but who yet believe that paradise, not concentration camps, await them in the twentieth century.

Out of the American melting pot of poverty, freedom, and opportunity—as exemplified by New York's Lower East Side at the turn of the century—arose a new American Jewish society of future Nobel prize winners, artists and statesmen who made the headlines of the world.

30

The Intellectual Giants

Was this paradise?

The Jews could hardly believe their senses. They had stepped out of sixteenth-century ghettos right into the nineteenth century and actually had been welcomed by the Christians. Western Europe seemed to be saturated with the philosophy of the age of reason launched by French thinkers such as Rousseau, Voltaire, Montesquieu, Diderot.

The social message of the French philosophers was very simple. Reason, they said, is a better guide to justice than God. Abolish religion, they advised; elevate reason to the throne of God, and human nature will change from evil to good.

And it seemed that these philosophers of the superiority of reason over faith might be right. The new Enlightenment held out its arms to the Jews who gratefully grabbed hold of them to be yanked into freedom.

Jews now fought as French Jews side by side with French Christians against the restoration of the Bourbons. They flocked to the banners of Italian Christians fighting to free Italy from its foreign oppressors, and called themselves Italian Jews. In Austria and Germany they joined the democratic forces fighting reaction and called themselves Austrian and German Jews. "We are part of the world again," the Jews exulted.

After three centuries of ghetto life, Western Europe seemed like a vast source of intellectual wonders to the emancipated Jews. There was not only Talmud and Torah for those Jews who wished them, but also science, philosophy, mathematics, art, music—all for the asking. All one needed to get ahead was to study and study and study some more, and be a little better than the next individual.

Hungrily, the emancipated children of the ghetto threw themselves into the world of Western civilization, studied avidly to master the arts and professions denied them for three centuries by Christian fanatics and Jewish fundamentalists.

Within one generation, and still within the shadow of the ghetto walls, the descendants of former Sabbateans, Frankists, Hasidism, Talmudists, and Cabalists became generals, statesmen, and avant-garde scholars who helped shape the modern world.

Christian genius produced Hegel, Spencer, and Darwin; Jewish genius produced Marx, Freud, and Einstein. The world viewed the art of Christian painters like Renoir, Cézanne, Gauguin, and Van Gogh; but it also viewed the art of Jewish painters like Modigliani, Soutine, Pissarro, and Chagall.

From King David to the Baal Shem Tov there had been no Jewish musicians of note; suddenly the world acclaimed the compositions of Felix Mendelssohn, Offenbach, Meyerbeer, and Mahler. Jews performed on Europe's concert stages, conducted orchestras of renown, and pioneered new art forms.

The heirs of the Talmud extended the frontiers of physics, mathematics, medicine, and chemistry. They snatched fifteen percent of the Nobel Prizes from the hands of the ruling Christian elite in spite of the fact that they represented but one percent of the total European and American population.

In mathematics Georg Kantor evolved the concept of transfinite numbers and outlined an approach to set theory. Carl Jacobi founded modern mathematical physics and developed the theories of elliptic and Abelian functions. Tullio Levi-Cevita with Gregory Ricci formulated absolute differential calculus and made possible the mathematics of general relativity. Herman Minkowski was the first to formulate the relativity of time and space.

Theoretical physics became so much a Jewish brainchild that the Germans derisively called it Judenphysik, Jew physics. Jewish physicists were the first to investigate photoelectric phenomena, and discover the Hertzian waves. They worked in electron kinetics, and isolated isotopes.

The Jews also founded the school of relativity—innovated by Albert Einstein—which led to the splitting of the atom and the development of the first atomic bomb. It was a Jewish trail all the way, beginning with Lise Meitner and her theory of nuclear fission, preceeding to Enrico Fermi and Leo Szilard who developed the chain reaction system, continuing to Niels Bohr who investigated the structure of the atom, and finally returning to Albert Einstein who convinced a skeptical President Franklin Delano Roosevelt of the idea that an atomic superbomb could be made. It is ironic—and frightening—to contemplate that, had Hitler not been so rabidly anti-Semitic, the Germans might have made the first atomic bomb and probably ruled the world by now.

In medicine, Jews laid the foundation for modern heart therapy. They discovered the serum immunity for contagious diseases, and made blood transfusion possible by discovering the different blood-types. The first hope for mankind for a cure against the ravages of venereal disease was the gift of three Jewish physicians—Neisser, Waserman, and Ehrlich—who isolated the causative germs and developed the first treatments.

In the field of politics, the Jewish achievement was equally impressive. In England, Benjamin Disraeli was named prime minister, and Sir Rufus Isaacs was elevated to viceroy of India. In France, Emile Pereiri built the country's first railroad, and Adolphe Cremieux became the minister of justice who abolished slavery in the French colonies and ended the death penalty for political prisoners. In Germany, Jews served with distinction as cabinet ministers, Reichstag members, and chief justices. They became industrialists of renown who helped elevate Germany to the rank of a first-class power.

Yet, amidst all these achievements, there were voices warning of future disaster. A great debate developed toward the end of the nineteenth century among the Jews. There were the optimists who claimed that the new age which had dawned was here to stay, and the pessimists who claimed that the Jews dwelled in a false paradise.

The optimists said, "Look at what we have achieved in five decades since our emancipation from the ghettos! We are no longer outsiders, but are a part of each community. Time has shown that the French philosophers were right. It was the church that banished us into ghettos because we would not give up our religion. But the world has changed. It no longer cares what religion anyone' believes in. Reason is neutral. Sure, there are still vestiges of the old anti-Semitism. But you know how it is—old prejudices die hard. New generations will be born without the prejudices of the past. We have nothing to fear except our own false prophets of gloom and doom."

And the pessimists said, "Something new, something terrifying is shaping itself on the political horizon. It is a new anti-Semitism of the state, far more deadly than the old anti-Jewishness of the church. It harbors the new disease of racism, which is already infecting the continent. The old test of *limpieza de sangre* of medieval Spain is being modernized by the state as a political weapon. Soon it won't be your religion that will count, but your blood. Soon the solution will not be the old formula of convert the Jews but a new state-inspired, anti-Semitic formula of kill the Jews. Today these voices only represent a minority. Tomorrow it will be the world."

Who was right, the optimists or the pessimists? It would take the Jews and the world another half-century, until World War II, to perceive the danger to all humanity of state-fostered anti-Semitism. But until then, the spirit of the poet Omar Kayyam prevailed—"Unborn tomorrow, dead yesterday, why fret about it when today is sweet."

The Jews at the turn of the nineteenth century, however, were confronted with another problem—the clear and present danger of assimilation. As the Jews soared into stardom in the firmament of Western civilization, they began to lose touch with Judaism. History had hurled them from the culture of ghetto isolationism to the culture of democratic pluralism. Judaism had either to compete in the marketplace of ideas or be in danger of becoming an anachronistic religion.

But this, as we have seen, was nothing new in Jewish history. When Judaism faced a similar crisis in the Greco-Roman world, we saw the Tannaim gallop to the rescue. In the challenge of the Parthian-Sassanid civilization, the Amoraim were the heroes. In the Islamic period, the Geonim were the survival experts. And in Renaissance days, we saw the Jews rescued by the Poskim.

Will Jewish history again come to the rescue of the Jews? Will history send new experts—a new set of Diaspora designers to meet the survival needs of the modern age? Does Jewish history still have a trick or two up its sleeve, or is it getting too old to meet new challenges? Will the luck of the Jews hold out?

We already have the answer. Jewish history, still alive and doing well, sent out new squads of experts to appraise the needs of the Jews in the modern age. The consensus was that in an age of pluralism, Judaism had to be pluralistic too.

The recommendations of those survival teams are still in an experimental stage. One rescue team advocated Reform Judaism; another proposed the modernization of Orthodoxy; others outlined ideas that led to Conservative Judaism and Reconstructionism. None has become dominant; yet all have been successful to some degree, for though assimilation and intermarriage continued, the tide away from Judaism was stemmed.

Tragedy and grandeur await the Jews in their Fourth Adventure. That drama transpired in one century on four stages—in Russia where the Jews are led to betrayal by czars and commissars; in the United States, which becomes the new Diaspora center for the world's Jews; in Germany where a new barbarism leads to the murder of six million Jews. The fourth stage is again Jerusalem—the Jews, betrayed by Western civilization, take to arms like the Maccabees of old, and reestablish an independent state of Israel.

31
Jews, Czars, and Commissars

The history of the Jews in Russia begins like a comedy and ends in tragedy.

The first Jews arrived in Southern Russia about 2,500 years ago as refugees from their defeats at the hands of the Assyrians, the Babylonians, and the Romans, respectively. When the Swedish Vikings, known as Rus (from which stems the name Russians) oared their way from the Baltic to Kiev on the Black Sea, the Jews were there to greet them.

Historic Russia, however, was not born until the tenth century C.E., when the Duke of Kiev defeated the Vikings and began his drive toward Moscow. Little is known of the Jews in Russia until the sixteenth century when they reenter Russian history with one of those sit-coms only Jews can produce.

Two Russian Jews who had been forcibly converted to Christianity began preaching Judaism to the muszhiks—the peasants—who liked it and converted to Judaism in droves. The Russian church, however, did not like it. The Jews were expelled with instructions not to come back.

The Jews did not come back on their own; they were hauled back. With one of the many annexations of Lithuania, Russia acquired more Jews in the seventeenth century than she had expelled in the sixteenth. So the Russians expelled them again.

But that did not help. When Czar Peter the Great wrested the Baltic provinces from Sweden, Russia again acquired twice as many Jews as she had previously had. Czar Peter did not expel them but his successors did.

The Russians acted, not out of anti-Semitism but out of xenophobia—a fear of foreigners. They expelled everybody who was not a Russian of the Greek Orthodox Christian persuasion—Roman Catholics, Protestants, Mohammedans, Jews, pagans. In fact, Empress Elizabeth, daughter of Peter the Great, persecuted Mohammedans with far greater dedication than she did Jews. At her orders, four hundred and eighteen of four hundred and thirty-six mosques in one province were burned, usually with the worshippers inside.

But Empress Catherine the Great (1762–1796) created her own Jewish problem. After she went into partnership with Austria and Prussia in carving up Poland, her slice contained nine-hundred thousand Jews. It is said she cried as Poland was partitioned, but she took her slice nevertheless.

We are now confronted with the question, How and when did so many Jews get to Poland? Jews were there as early as the ninth century C.E. But who these early Polish Jews were is still a mystery. Some aver they were the refugees from the former kingdom of Khazar after its defeat by the Duke of Kiev.* These mystery Jews were joined in the twelfth century by Jews from Western Europe fleeing the Rhineland one step ahead of the Crusaders.

Polish kings welcomed the Jews fleeing the West, for the same reasons the crowned heads of Western Europe had welcomed them previously—to stimulate the economy. Polish kings granted the Jews charters of self-government, and the Jews helped found new towns and industries. They prospered, owned property, and built beautiful synagogues. One Gothic-style synagogue in Cracow, built in the thirteenth century, was restored after World War II by the Polish communist government and declared a cultural monument.

This golden age lasted for close to three centuries, until calamity overtook Poles and Jews when Greek Orthodox cossacks invaded Poland. Their cruelty knew no limits. The enemy was the Polish nobility who had exploited them, the German merchants who had cheated them, the Polish peasants because they were Roman Catholics, and the Jews because they were there. After the cossacks came the Swedes who further mutilated the bleeding body of Poland.

Finally, after the departure of the Swedes, the three rulers sitting on the thrones of Russia, Prussia, and Austria deemed it safe to partition the Polish cadaver among themselves. And now Empress Catherine the Great of Russia was faced with a dilemma—what to do with the nine-hundred thousand Jews she had acquired with her slice of Poland.

Though Catherine's sense of decency did not permit her to wantonly expel that many Jews, her sense of rulership told her the Jews of Poland could not be absorbed into Russia itself without causing problems. She hit upon an ingenious solution. The Jews already in Russia proper could remain where they were. But Russia itself would be off limits to the Jews of Poland. Toward this end, she made Poland and the Baltic countries into one vast ghetto which she named the Pale of Settlement, or simply the

---

*Arthur Koestler, in his book, *The Thirteenth Tribe*, gives a fascinating, though unhistoric, account of the Polish Jews being the descendants of the Khazars.

Pale. Here, with a few exceptions, the Jews could move at will. Here bloomed the shtetls, the small rural towns.

Soon three distinct Jewish social classes emerged in the Russian empire—a small, well-to-do intellectual elite living mostly in the cities of Russia itself, a large mass of urban Jews living in the cities of Poland and Lithuania, and the largest mass—the rural Jews dwelling in the shtetls of the Pale.

Five Romanov czars dominated the nineteenth century. Their incompetence paved the way for disaster. Anything they gave was too little and too late, and anything they took away was too much, too soon. Serfs received freedom, but no land. Torture was officially abolished, but the people had too little political freedom. The czars preached enlightenment, but the masses were kept illiterate. Both Jews and Russians were the victims of these policies.

The fault was not entirely that of the czars. No sooner had a czar announced a liberal policy than the nobles and clergy opposed it; no sooner was a more conservative policy enacted than the radicals rebelled. In one century this policy of vacillation pushed Russia from the brink of democracy into communism.

Russia was sick unto her Slavic soul. To cure herself, Russia took a brand of aspirin known as slavophilism; that is, a rabid love for anything Slavic. The new slogan was "One creed, one czar, and one fatherland." Konstantin Pobedonostsev (1827–1907), put in charge of the "Jewish question," came up with the formula "One-third conversion, one-third emigration, and one-third starvation." A series of pogroms—a Russian word standing for state-inspired persecution—was instituted against the Jews. This turned Jewish life in Russia into a nightmare, triggering a mass migration of some 2,500,000 Jews to the United States between 1880 and 1920.

Within a few decades, the Pobedonostsev formula was to be adopted by other totalitarian states to solve their problems of unwanted population segments. Indeed, that formula was applied in recent times by the Vietnamese communists to the Cambodians—one segment converted to communism, another segment forced to become boat people, and a third segment left to starve.

It was not just the Jews but the entire Russian population who suffered. In disgust the Russian people one day in 1881 blew up their beloved Little Father Czar Alexander II. But it changed nothing.

Nicholas II, the last of the Romanovs, took Russia into anarchy with his stupidities, which included giving the Russian people a taste of bullets instead of bread. In response, he reaped the Communist Revolution (1917) and death against a blood-spattered wall in the Ekaterineburg prison in Siberia.

But that did not help either. The Russian people got something worse than the Romanovs—the rule of the communist commissars. They got

Lenin and Stalin who in four decades murdered more Russians than all the czars had done in five centuries.

The communists changed the czarist formula vis-à-vis the Jews to one-half converted to communism and one-half doomed to extinction through the deprivation of all human rights." In Russia today, the life of the Jews as Jews has literally come to a dead end.

32
Jews and Yanks

Was it prophetic that in 1492, the year Spain expelled the Jews, Columbus set sail for America? That the Jews were among the first to settle in the new continent? That the Jews were drawn to the thirteen colonies and to the Puritans who believed they were Israelites? And it is also prophetic that the United States was destined to become the largest, most important, Disapora center in Jewish history?

American Jewish history began inconspicuously one September day in 1654, when twenty-three poverty-stricken Jews arrived on a French ship in the harbor of the Dutch colony of New Amsterdam, where they were dumped by the captain of the ship.

Where did they come from and why?

Jewish history seldom has simple answers, and certainly not in this instance. The story starts with the discovery of Brazil in 1500. A Marrano buccaneer named Fernando de Loronha undertook to explore the coast of Brazil for Portugal, provided the king would permit the Jews to settle there. Permission granted, de Loronha set sail for Brazil. In 1503 his Marranos built the first fort on Brazilian soil in the name of King Manuel, their oppressor.

Jewish settlements grew rapidly in Brazil, Surinam, Barbados, Martinique, Curacao, Jamaica. The Jews engaged in extensive world trade and prospered—until Portugal and Spain set up branch offices of the Inquisition in the New World. It now became a game of life and death to stay one step ahead of the Inquisition.

When the city of Recife in Brazil was recaptured by the Portuguese from the Dutch in 1654, the Jews fled in sixteen ships for Holland. Fifteen ships made it. The sixteenth, sunk by Spanish pirates, was captured by a French barque. The Jews were freed, but because they had no money with which to pay for their passage to Holland, the captain abandoned them in the nearest port, which happened to be New Amsterdam. They promptly were told by the town's choleric governor, Peter Stuyvesant, to get out because there was no place here for such riffraff. The Jews refused, claiming they were Dutch citizens.

Stuyvesant did not confine his prejudices to Jews. He was a bigot of immense capacities, with tolerance only for members of his own Dutch

Reformed Church. Just before the arrival of the Jews, he had banned Lutherans from settling in town and had ordered Catholics to be flogged. And now fate put twenty-three Portuguese Jews in his front yard.

Seething with indignation, Stuyvesant wrote a letter to his employers, the Dutch West India Company in Amsterdam, asking for permission to send "these blasphemers of Christ" back where they came from. He was stunned when the reply stated that the Jews be allowed to stay and trade, provided they would support themselves and not become a burden to the community.

Reluctantly Stuyvesant complied. Undaunted, the Jews went to work. Seven years later, after the British ousted the Dutch, the Jews became British subjects. At this point American Judaism took off in a different direction from European Judaism. The two main reasons for this were the Puritan spirit and an amendment to the Constitution.

The British ruling class had viewed the Puritans in England as Jewish fellow travellers. When the Puritans departed for the colonies, the British thought of the event as good riddance to bad rubbish.

The Puritans considered themselves as Israelites. They modeled their new homeland in the wilderness on the principles of the Old Testament. They looked upon their flight from England as the flight of the Israelites from Egypt. They strewed New England with Hebrew place-names and they observed as strict a Sabbath as did the Jews, although on Sunday. Hebrew was taught at Harvard when it was founded, and it almost became the language of Massachusetts. And Governor Cotton Mather at one time wanted to make the code of Moses the law of that colony. This spirit of Puritanism hovered over the continent for two centuries, and the Jews felt right at home in America.

But it was the First Amendment to the Constitution that was to have the most profound impact on the future of American Judaism. It states: "Congress shall make no law respecting the establishment of religion, or prohibiting the exercise thereof."

With that amendment, there was no way in which a religious law could be enforced by anyone—priest, rabbi, or president. An offender against a religious teaching could be kicked out of a church or synagogue, but not put in prison.

For the American Jew it meant that Judaism, like any other religion in America, could not be forced on anyone. Thus, Judaism became voluntary. And it showed that Judaism was strong enough to survive through choice alone, without force.

There were several other reasons that also influenced the independent course American Judaism took. Because the Portuguese and Spanish Jews, who were the first Jews to settle in the colonies, had never had a ghetto tradition, they wore the same clothes the Christians did. Thus, in looks, the Jews were indistinguishable from the Christian colonists and mingled freely with them.

Because the Jews could get justice in American courts, they did not need courts of their own. Therefore, most Jewish institutions of the old world vanished on American soil. About the only institutions that survived were the synagogue and cemetery.

But the synagogue, too, underwent drastic changes. Because there were very few permanent ordained rabbis in the United States for the first two-hundred years, it was difficult for the European rabbinic system to establish itself on American soil.

Because of this shortage of rabbis, any Jew with a smattering of knowledge of Hebrew was usually appointed preacher of his synagogue. As he had no rabbinic training, he had to innovate. These innovations in turn led to the psychological acceptance of change in ritual, custom, and tradition.

The most famed of such innovating preachers was Mendes Seixas (1746–1816). He gave Thanksgiving Day sermons, spoke before Christian audiences, lectured in colleges. He became the forerunner of today's American-Jewish spiritual leader, a type unknown until then in Jewish history.

The colonial and Sephardi period came to an end with the American Revolution. Jews fought on the side of both Whigs and Tories—preponderantly, however, on the side of Washington.

The revolution freed only half of the people. Of the total population in 1776 (not counting Indians), thirty percent were black slaves, and twenty percent were white indentured servants.* But all Jews were free, since no Jew was a slave or an indentured servant.

New waves of immigration (most of German origin) from 1820 to 1880 swelled the Jewish population from 25,000 to 250,000. The German Jews did not stay long on the eastern seaboard, but funneled through the Cumberland Gap to all points west—to Cincinnati, Cleveland, Louisville, St. Louis, New Orleans. The Oregon fever and the gold rush swept them with the "forty-niner" elite to the Pacific coast by 1850.

The slavery issue divided the Jews just as it did the Christians. Like the Southern Christians, so the Southern Jews fought not so much for slavery as out of love for the South. The Confederacy gave the Jews their first statesman, Judah P. Benjamin, who served as Secretary of War under Confederate President Jefferson Davis.

After the Civil War, the German Jews went into banking and retailing, making great fortunes in these fields. A new class of elitist Jew emerged—the "merchant prince." But what a vast difference there was between the European medieval prince and the Jewish merchant prince. Whereas the former used wealth to fill his castles with works of art to be beheld by nobles of equal rank, the Jewish merchant prince donated millions to museums, funded orchestras, and established chairs in the sciences and humanities. He gave millions to fund networks of Jewish hospitals, Jewish old age homes, and social welfare programs for the poor.

---

*Indentured servitude; as an institution, died out in the United States by 1820.

In 1881 the dam broke for the third and largest immigration wave of Jews, radically changing the demographic composition of the American Jews. That was the year the Russian Jews came, not as isolated individuals but as families, entire villages, towns. They came by the tens of thousands each month. By 1920 there were almost three million Russians and East European Jews.

The vast majority of these East European Jews arrived penniless. Those having skills found immediate employment. Those having none took either to the peddler's tray, or opened hole-in-the-wall enterprises— tailor shops, grocery and hardward stores, candy stalls. But few looked upon these occupations as permanent. To them America was the *goldene medina*—the land of golden opportunities which would give their children, if not them, the chance for a place in the economic sun.

And thus these immigrants worked from sunup to sundown, saving pennies to send their children to America's "baptismal fonts"—public schools and colleges. Education was the secret word for success. Within a generation, the children of these former denizens of ghettos and shtetls, soared into American headlines.

An American Jew, Albert Abraham Michelson, famed for his studies in measuring the velocity of light, became America's first Nobel Prize winner (1907); Isidor Rabin won acclaim and a Nobel Prize for his research in quantum mechanics; Herman Joseph Muller received his Nobel medal for his artificial transmutation of genes through X-rays.

In medicine, Selman Waksman isolated streptomycin; Casimir Funk discovered vitamins; and Jonas Salk introduced the first vaccine against polio.

A generation after the arrival of the Russian Jews, Jewish political and cultural activities exploded. Suddenly there appeared five Jewish Supreme Court Justices in quick succession, a host of governors and senators, cabinet members and advisors who won fame in jurisprudence and politics. Jewish conductors, musicians, and playwrights dominated stage and screen. Jews composed the songs Americans hummed, wrote the novels the world read, made movies the world viewed. American Jews became sculptors, artists, art critics of world renown.

But even more. In the twentieth century, America became the main Diaspora center. In this century, the American Jews entered the international arena of Jewish world affairs. They helped secure the Palestine mandate at the peace negotiations after World War I; they helped secure an independent state of Israel at the United Nations in 1948; they helped Israel survive the initial shocks a new independent state is heir to. In every phase of Jewish international life, American Jews occupy seats of leadership.

The ferment and change in the field of religion was as great as that in the fields of economics and politics. America had become a vast experimental laboratory for new forms of Judaism. We saw the colonial Sephardi Jews discard most of their European institutions and develop new American ideas to take their place. When the English and German Jews arrived after the Revolution, they in turn were influenced by the institutions already established by their Sephardi predecessors. We witnessed the birth of frontier Judaism, a Judaism played by ear, but which nevertheless endured by the sheer will of the Jews to survive as Jews. Next we saw the emergence of voluntary Judaism, a Judaism which could not be enforced by state or synagogue, but nevertheless was accepted by choice.

By 1800, Judaism was a religion in search of leaders to give it unity and purpose as it spread across the continent. New challenges were assailing the faith of the Jews as the ever restless frontier sucked them further and further West, further and further away from their roots in Europe. There was a danger the link would snap.

To keep the continuity of the Judaism, which was emerging on the American frontier Diaspora, with its European past, history again sent one of its improbable rescue teams—composed this time of an American-born Sephardi playwright and three Ashkenzai scholars from the hinterland of Europe. They were Isaac Harby (1788–1828) of Charleston, South Carolina, a misfit on the Jewish scene who by a fluke of history mulched the soil for the coming reforms in American Judaism; Bohemian-born Rabbi Isaac Mayer Wise (1819–1900), who became the father of American Reform Judaism by transplanting German Reform onto ante-bellum Judaism; Rumanian-born Solomon Schechter (1850–1915), a lecturer in Talmudics in Cambridge, England, from whose scholarly brow sprang Coservative Judaism; and Lithuanian-born Bernard Revel (1885–1940), who, after making it in the oilfields of Oklahoma, transformed European-style Orthodoxy into an American brand.

Isaac Harby had studied law, then successively became a novelist, essayist, and playright, but failed financially in all his professions and died in abject poverty. His *shlemielship* pursued him even after death. Till this date, history has still given him scant credit for his one remarkable achievement.

Repelled by the synagogue customs of his time, which still reflected ghetto customs, Harby, on impulse, founded the first reform temple in America, The Reformed Society of Israelites, in 1824. Its innovations gained the attention of President Thomas Jefferson who wrote to Harby stating that while, "I am little acquainted with the liturgy of the Jews or their mode of worship . . . nothing is wiser than that all our institutions should keep the advance with time."

Though Harby's Reformed Society lasted but nine years, his ideas sparked great interest. By 1846, the year Rabbi Wise stepped off the gangplank in New York with a wife, a child, and no money or passport, there were already three Reform temples in America.

The career of Rabbi Wise was launched in 1850, during the Rosh Hashana services, with a punch in the nose by the president of the Orthodox Congregation Beth El in Albany, New York, where Wise, as its rabbi, had been introducing Reform too rapidly. The fight which ensued spilled out in the streets and had to be broken up by the police.

Undaunted, Wise accepted another post in Cincinnati. But, having learned caution from his previous experience, he now launched Reform Judaism into American homes through the portals of diplomacy and reason. In the four decades that followed, American Judaism was largely that of Reform Judaism as Wise conceived it. By 1880, of the two hundred largest congregations, only eight were orthodox. His greatest achievements were the establishment of the Union of American Hebrew Congregations, the first cohesive Jewish religious body in America, and the founding of the first successful rabbinic college in the United States which also became the first in Jewish history to ordain women.

However, parallel with the rise of Reform, many Jews felt that Reform was travelling away from Orthodoxy a bit too fast. Feeling comfortable neither with Reform nor Orthodoxy, this discontented segment of Jews solved its problem in a typical American fashion. They founded a new sect of Judaism and called it Conservative.

The new sect, however, had no formal creed and few members. Casting about for a personality who could flesh out a Conservative creed, attract new members, shore up the sagging fortunes of their newly founded Jewish Theological Seminary in New York and promote Jewish scholarship, the choice fell upon the right man into achieve these miracles—Solomon Schechter. After having enriched his yeshiva education with several university degrees, Schechter had become Lecturer of Talmudics at Cambridge, England, where he won local fame with his wit and learning, and world fame for having identified some fragments as part of an ancient manuscript of Ecclesiasticus.

Surrounding himself with distinguished scholars, Schechter succeeded in making Conservative Judaism a potent force among American Jews. Instead of fitting American-Jewish aspirations into a Procrustean* bed of European concepts of Judaism, he defty steered a Conservative path between Reform and Orthodoxy.

Thus it was this Reform and Conservative Judaism that greeted the three million largely Orthodox Jews who were drawn from Eastern Europe to American shores in the four decades between 1880 and 1920. But instead of this three-million immigrant majority of European Orthodox Jews influencing the 250,000 American Jewish minority, the reverse happened. The American brands of Judaism made such an impact on the children of the immigrants, that Orthodoxy was forced to modernize itself to retain the religious affiliations of its children.

The Orthodox stage was now set for the fourth member of the rescue team—Bernard Revel, the man from Lithuania who, after a stint in the oilfields of Oklahoma, returned to the New York educational scene to

---

*In Greek mythology, Procrustes was an inkeeper who had but one bed into which each guest had to fit. If too long for the bed, the guest's legs were chopped off; if too short, the body was stretched to fit. The bed was never wrong; only the body.

reform European Orthodoxy. Seeing no danger in combining Judaism with science, he med two dilapidated New York yeshivas into one successful school where Orthodox students could study the Talmud and the worldly philosophers without a split in loyalties. The school grew in prestige, and with time became Yeshiva College, then Yeshiva University, the first Jewish liberal arts institutions in the United States. Revel's successor added the Albert Einstein College of Medicine with a faculty not only of Jews (which includes Reform and Conservative), but non-Jews as well.

American Jews could now ordain their own rabbis without having to import them from Europe, and with the establishment of their own university presses—the Hebrew Union College, the Jewish Theological Seminary, and Yeshiva University—could compete with the scholarship of European Jews and eventually surpass them.

The American Jewish experimental laboratory for new varieties of religious experience did not close its doors with the successes of Reform, Conservative, and modern Orthodoxy. Here, in this laboratory was also born organizational Judaism, another uniquely American product. In America, Judaism speaks not only through its rabbis, synagogues, and temples, but also through its organizations—Jewish Federations, United Jewish Appeal, B'nai Brith, National Council of Jewish Women, Hadassah, Jewish Community Centers Association, ORT, American Jewish Committee, American Jewish Congress, and many, many others.

All these organizations, totally American in origin, (with the exception of ORT, founded in Europe), have been adopted by Diaspora Jews the world over, and Israel too. All serve to help the Jews grapple with the Jewish problems on a world-wide stage. American Judaism thinks universalist Judaism.

In 1831 a Frenchman named Alexis deTocqueville visited America, and in 1835 published a remarkable book, *Democracy in America*. Unlike other European historians, he saw beyond the dirty fingernails and bad manners of pre-Civil War America. He predicted that in another century the United States would be the arsenal of democracy in the world. The world of 1850 laughed at him.

If there were such a deTocqueville visiting America today, writing a book on American Judaism, what would he see?

Would he see the end of Judaism as Jews forsake the ghetto ways of their grandparents, and seemingly take themselves out of Judaism via intermarriage and creeping assimilationism?

Or would he see those manifestations as mere surface phenomena? Would he see instead a renaissance, a reawakening of Judaism in America—Jews shedding former European ghetto wrappings, searching for new roots in their amazing past, affirming the eternal values of Judaism while hurrying for a rendezvous with destiny? Would he see the emerging American Judaism as the coming international phase of Judaism—a spectrum from Orthodoxy to Reform?

Future history will give us the answer.

33

The Nazi Pimps

On January 20, 1933, Adolph Hitler became chancellor of Germany. This event released a new age of barbarism in Europe.

From that day until April 1945, when Germany surrendered in World War II, the Nazis murdered in cold blood thirteen million civilians—men, women, and children—by firing squads, starvation, and poison gas. Six million were Jews; seven million were Christians. Too late the world realized that at peril were not only the Jews but humanity itself.

But how could such an infamy happen in Germany, viewed by many as culturally the most advanced nation in the world?

The tide of her cultural advance had turned with Germany's defeat in World War I. Her behavior in defeat was ignominious. German sailors mutinied; German soldiers threw down their guns and ran. The kaiser, who had sworn to die for the fatherland, fled to Holland begging for asylum. And, rather than admit they had been beaten fair and square, the Germans whined they had been stabbed in the back. As Winston Churchill so contemptuously characterized this German behavior: "The Hun is either at your throat or at your feet."

The Weimar republic which replaced the kaiser was governed by weak men who, under the pretense of democracy, permitted left- and right-wing organizations of hatred to undermine it. In less than a decade, terrorists on both sides murdered over three hundred prominent men in public office—Catholics, Protestants, Jews.

In this atmosphere of lawlessness, a jobless house painter named Adolph Hitler staged, in 1922, his now famous *putsch* in Munich to overthrow the German government. Arrested, Hitler was given a five-year sentence of which he served but one. Within ten years after his release from prison, he became the sole ruler of Germany, with absolute power.

Who was this pimp of sadism who murdered his way into history? Adolph Hitler's father was the illegitimate son of a vagrant; his mother was a peasant girl, twenty-three years younger than her husband. Hitler himself was an undistinguished student, an undistinguished soldier, and unsuccessful house painter, and an artist without talent. But he was a brilliant politician with hypnotic oratorical powers who could sway his audiences into a frenzy of hate.

The West greatly underestimated him, especially his honesty. In his book *Mein Kampf*, Hitler told the world that he would kill the Jews, and he did. He wrote that he would lie, cheat, and resort to war to achieve his ends, and he did. He wrote he would invade Poland and Russia, and all other Slavic countries, and subjugate them to slave labor status to serve the German people, and he did. Not until it was too late did the world believe him.

From 1933 to 1939, Hitler achieved all his political aims without firing a shot. He repudiated the Versailles treaty, rearmed Germany, annexed the Rhineland, occupied Austria, took the Sudetenland, invaded Czechoslovakia—all in plain view of the "peace-makers" of Europe who, headed by Neville Chamberlain, proclaimed that all Hitler wanted was peace.

As soon as Hitler was in the political saddle, he set out to organize Germany for brutality and war. With the Nuremberg laws of 1935, he disenfranchised all Jews, stripping them of their professions and businesses. Until 1939, they were allowed to leave Germany upon payment of huge ransoms, and three-hundred thousand of Germany's six-hundred thousand Jews fled.

But the Nazis wanted to obliterate Christianity as well. They saw Christianity as a danger because, in their view, it weakened the Aryan strain of blood by admitting people of all races within its fold. Nazi doctrine held that Hitler, not Jesus, was the true savior.

The first concentration camps were built not for Jews but for Christians. To discredit religion, priests and ministers were brought to trial on immorality charges. They were among the first to be sent to concentration camps along with communists, socialists, republicans, and ordinary Germans who believed in democracy and opposed Hitler.

Hitler had three fantasies. One was to conquer Europe for himself and then divide the rest of the world with Japan. The second was to kill the Jews. The third was to exterminate all Slavic people not needed to serve Germany. With the start of World War II, he began to implement these three fantasies.

For the first time in the history of mankind we see a country organize a corps of intellectuals to draft blueprints for mass murder at union wages. In no civilization except that of Nazi Germany have efficiency experts been employed to devise plans for the profitable disposal of the by-products of corpses. Germans bought mattresses stuffed with hair shaved from corpses, ate vegetables fertilized with ashes from incinerated cadavers, washed their faces with soap made from the fatty acids of boiled bodies—all for the greater profit of *das Vaterland.*

The task of killing civilians according to plan was first entrusted to murder squads called *Einsatzgruppen.* Persons doomed to death were lined along ditches they had been forced to dig, then machine-gunned. Bulldozers finished the job.

To speed up this murder program, the concentration camps of the 1930s were modernized with spigots for poison gas and ovens for burning those murdered. Within four years, three million Jews perished at the hands of the *Einsatzgruppen* and three million were gassed to death. These killings were euphemistically termed "the final solution."

Behind the final solution for the Jews was another final solution for those Christians deemed subhuman by the Germans—Poles, Russians, Ukrainians, Lithuanians, Latvians, Estonians—people the German masters had decreed were in excess of the number needed to serve the German state. For these Christians a cheaper and more practical method of disposal was used. Because the Germans viewed these Christians as subhuman with low intelligence, they deemed it safe enough to first exploit them as slave laborers until they lost their economic usefulness. The average life of a slave laborer in Germany was three months. Then the person was sent to a concentration camp to die, usually of starvation.

After the war, some historians hypocritically asked the question, "Why didn't the Jews fight back?" implying that everyone else except the Jews did fight back. Let us dig a little further into this question.

Three million Russian prisoners of war were deliberately starved to death in their prison compounds by Germans as part of a program to reduce the Russian population. Nobody asked why these three million Russian prisoners did not fight back. They were soldiers, trained to fight, yet they did not. Passively in their prison compounds they waited, and died from hunger and cold.

At Bataan, seventy thousand American soldiers surrendered to the Japanese, after which the notorious Bataan death march began. Only a few thousand Japanese guarded them, yet history tells us the American soldiers did not fight back. Yet no one asks why not.

We know that the seven million Christians exterminated by the Nazi—three million East European civilians, one million miscellaneous Christians from Western Europe, and three million Russian prisoners of war—did not fight back.

But what about the Jews?

Of all the people imprisoned by the Nazis, only the Jews fought back. ᵔᵛ fought not only in the ghetto of Warsaw, but in ghettos throughout Europe; and they joined underground movements. But the moment Jews joined the underground, lo and behold, a miracle took place. They were classified as Poles, Greeks, Russians, Italians, French, Dutch—but never as Jews. Alexander Wirth, author of the epic work *Russia at War*, states that a large segment of the members of the Russian underground were Jews.

The uprising in the Warsaw ghetto was a turning point in Jewish history. The truth dawned not only on the Jews in Warsaw but on Jews all over the world. The early Zionists had been right. The anti-Semitism of the state was not a political opinion but an irrational, pathological condition; and it was absurd to think that this kind of mental aberration could be cured with reason. The Jews of Warsaw did not turn the other cheek. They fought the Nazis—as the Russians, the French, the English, and the Americans finally did.

The population in the ghetto dwindled from 450,000 to 40,000 Jews as Nazi stormtroopers railroaded the Jews to concentration camps under the ruse that they were being taken to labor camps instead. One day, when eight hundred stormtroopers came to round up a new shipment of Jews, they were met with bullets and Molotov cocktails instead of supplication. The battle raged for three days. In the end, in utter disbelief, the Nazis were forced to retreat.

Fear swept Nazi ranks. The Jews had rebelled and flung them back. Though the Jews had only seven thousand men of fighting age, the Nazis pitted an entire division against them. The battle raged for six weeks—two weeks longer than it took Germany to conquer Poland. In the end, the Nazis won, but it was a Pyrrhic* victory, for they knew how high the cost had been. Suddenly the Germans realized that against the armed Jews, the Nazis were no longer supermen.

With 1945, World War II at last was coming to an end. The allies on the Western front crossed the Rhine River into Germany, and the Russians on the Eastern front drove eight million German soldiers back to their *Vaterland*. Hitler, seeing all was lost, shot himself in the mouth; the S.S. elite burned their uniforms like dung, hid themselves in civilian clothing, or else fell to their knees begging, "Kamerad, don't shoot." The biggest killing spree in the history of man—World War II, with a total of forty-seven million casualties—was over.

The irony, and the wonder, is that in spite of all the bloodshed and murder by the Nazis, they could not stop the march of Jewish history. Nazi Germany, which Hitler had vowed would last a thousand years, collapsed after twelve years. The Jews, whom Hitler swore he would exterminate, survived and marched on to create the new independent state of Israel.

---

*Pyrrhus, King of Epirus (295–272 B.C.E.), exclaimed after a costly victory with heavy losses over the Romans, "One more such a victory and I am lost."

III

Zionists to the Rescue (The Present)

The Jews, who have poured into Palestine under the impetus of Zionism, reach into the attic of their history to arm themselves with the shield of David and the sword of Bar Kochba to once again march under Jewish generals giving commands in Hebrew to reestablish, against all odds, a new Jewish state, the state of Israel.

From the attic of their history, the Jews took down the shield of David and the armor of bar Kochba, recreating in 1948 the State of Israel. In 1967, jubilant Israeli soldiers reunited Old and New Jerusalem into one Jerusalem, bringing King Solomon's Temple back into Jewish history.

34

The Road Back

In 1897 in Basel, Switzerland, the delegates to the first Zionist convention rose to give Theodor Herzl a standing ovation. He had called the convention and proposed that the Jews return to Palestine to establish an independent Jewish homeland.

That evening Herzl wrote in his diary, "In Basel I founded the Jewish state . . . . Maybe in five years, certainly in fifty, everybody will recognize it."

Herzl was wrong. It took fifty-one years.

But who was Theodor Herzl?

An event in Paris in 1893 catapulted Theodor Herzl on to the Jewish scene. It began with an aristocratic scoundrel named Ferdinand Esterhazy, a major in the French army who lived above his means. To supplement his income, he sold French military secrets to the Germans. Suspicion settled on a Captain Alfred Dreyfus because he was the only Jew on the French general staff. To its horror, the general staff discovered that Esterhazy, not Dreyfus, was the traitor. But how could they accuse a French aristocrat and career officer of espionage? It seemed too absurd. To guard itself against such an absurdity, an army court sentenced Dreyfus to life imprisonment on Devil's Island. There he would have rotted away but for a Catholic colonel named Georges Picquart who stumbled upon the truth. At the risk of his own career, Colonel Picquart went public with his findings.

A nationwide crisis erupted. France was divided into two camps—those for Dreyfus who demanded justice, and those against Dryfus who demanded death to all Jews as traitors. The hysteria grew, and wild street-fights developed.

Into the fracas stepped a world-famed French novelist named Emile Zola, who published a pamphlet entitled *J'Accuse*. In it he openly charged the French government with a frame-up of Dreyfus. Esterhazy confessed;

Dreyfus was exonerated, promoted to major, and given the Legion of Honor.

The story of Dreyfus himself is unimportant to Jewish history; what is important is that with the Dreyfus affair, political Zionism was born. Its founder, Theodor Herzl (1860–1904), was not the kind of messiah pious Jews had envisaged would lead them back to Zion.

Theodor Herzl, handsome and aristocratic, was born in Budapest, the son of a rich, partly-assimilated Jewish family. Admitted to the bar in Vienna, Herzl gave up law for a career in journalism. Sent by his newspaper to Paris to cover the Dreyfus affair, he threw himself into the fight to free the captain. Herzl, who at one time had toyed with the idea of converting to Christianity, was shocked into Jewishness when he heard the mob in the streets shout, "Death to the Jews!"

Almost overnight Herzl became the prophet of Zionism. In a short time he hammered out *The Jewish State*, the book that shook the Jewish world. He wrote: "The Jews who wish it, will have their own state. We shall at last live like free men on our own soil, die peacefully in our own beds. The world will be freed by our liberty, enriched by our wealth, magnified by our greatness."

The coming Zionist revolution had been sparked.

Herzl was a prophet in a hurry. He had no time for intellectual debates. He offered the Jews freedom, not in stages but in one daring stroke. He held out to them the image of the proud people they had once been; he had no place for the derided ghetto Jew. And the people loved him for it and shouted, "Long live Herzl, the king!" They wanted a messiah not in rags but in morning coat and striped trousers. They had had enough of rags in the ghetto.

Any sane man could have said in 1897 that Herzl was a nut, that his ideas would never succeed. They also could and did tick off a long list of "why not." There were only thirty-five thousand Jews in all Palestine; the country was a swampy, malaria-ridden wasteland; Hebrew had not been a spoken language for 1,700 years—one could not even ask for a cup of coffee in it. Besides, Palestine belonged to the Ottoman empire—and who was going to fight the Turks for the Jews?

The trouble with people of little faith is that they have no idea of the power of faith. It was faith in the Zionist idea that motivated 650,000 Jews from all over the world to settle in the Palestine of the Ottoman empire. They drained the swamps, ended malaria, and turned Palestine once again into a land of milk and honey.

A fanatic named Eliezer Ben-Yehuda went to Palestine and single-handedly shaped biblical Hebrew into a modern Hebrew so you could ask for "a cup of coffee with croissants, please" in that language.

Two more fanatics—a Jew named Vladimir Jabotinsky, a bohemian Russian drama critic, who had been thrown out of Odessa for abusing the police chief; and a Christian named Order Wingate, a British major general born with Old Testament prophecy in his bones—organized the Jews in Palestine into fighting units.

And finally, in 1917, a British peer, Lord Arthur James Balfour, issued a document bearing his name which declared: "His Majesty's Government view with favor the establishment in Palestine of a national home for the Jewish people."

Thus, a mere twenty years after the first Zionist congress in Basel, there existed a framework for a future independent Jewish state.

The guiding hand behind Lord Balfour and the Balfour Declaration was that of aristocratic Chaim Weizmann (1875–1952), a passionate Zionist and renowned chemist. Born in an obscure plot of mud named Mote near Minsk in Russia, Weizmann was educated in Talmudics in the Pale and in science at Swiss and German universities. In 1904 he was appointed lecturer in biological chemistry at the Manchester University in England, in 1916 he was named director of the British Admiralty chemical laboratories. It was here he made the momentous discovery that helped England win World War I.

German submarines were sinking boats carrying Chilean nitrates to England, desperately needed as a source of explosives. Weizmann found a way of producing acetone, an essential ingredient in the synthetic manufacture of such explosives, and turned his discovery over to the British. This brought him in contact with the highest personages in the British ministry, giving him the opportunity to interest many members in the Zionist cause, including Lord Balfour. When the draft of the Balfour Declaration was shown to Weizmann, he exclaimed, "We can hear the steps of the messiah."

The allies won World War I. The Ottoman empire surrendered, and Palestine was turned over to England as a mandate, consonant with the Balfour Declaration.

In the three decades of the mandate (1920–1948), the British showed their preference for the Arabs by doing their best to antagonize the Jews. In 1922, they partitioned Palestine in two, giving three-fourths of it—30,000 square miles out of 48,000—to the Arabs who created the kingdom of Transjordan, later renamed Jordan. They ignored the recommendation of their own Peel commission (1938) to partition what remained of Palestine into an Arab and Jewish state. They tried to freeze the Jews into a minority status by restricting Jewish, but not Arab, immigration. The Arabs, instead of embracing the British with loyalty for these favors, betrayed them by joining the Nazis in World War II against the British. But when the Arabs realized that their Nazi comrades were losing the war, they promptly switched their allegiance back to the British.

The chemistry of the Jews had meanwhile changed. The statistics of the Holocaust had proven to them that the philosophy of accommodation no longer worked. This was the time to fight back. No more holocausts—German or Arab.

Zionist history was now ready for a man of action to infuse the torrent of events into the Jewish dream of an independent state. That man was David Ben-Gurion (1886–1973), born in Plonsk, a dreary factory town in Poland. A rabid Zionist at age ten, he hitchhiked in 1906 to Palestine but was expelled by the Turks in 1915, as an Allied sympathizer. In 1918, when Adolph Hitler was a corporal in the German army, Ben-Gurion was a corporal in the Jewish brigade of the British army.

Ben-Gurion, tough and single-minded, stated his creed in thoughts like hammer blows—unlimited immigration, creation of a Jewish army, the unification of Palestine into an independent Jewish state. His message sank into the Jewish consciousness. Instead of turning the other cheek, the Jews began returning violence with violence. Neither the British nor the Arabs liked it. They had been accustomed to docile Jews. It was so easy to deal with that kind. Now, to their dismay, they discovered—like the Nazis during the Warsaw uprising—that against armed Jews they were no longer supermen.

The Jews now openly defied the British white paper that forbade Jewish emigration to Palestine. Surviving Jews of Europe sailed their leaky boats to Palestine right under the guns of the British. Fire was met with fire. Especially feared by the Arabs and the British was the Irgun, a Jewish underground organization that returned a tooth for a tooth, an eye for an eye, and a hanging for a hanging. But unlike the future Arab terrorist organizations, the Irgun only attacked armed soldiers, not civilians.

Anarchy erupted. In 1947 the British threw up their hands and asked the United Nations to take over the mandate. The United Nations voted to partition Palestine into an Arab and a Jewish state. The Jews accepted. The Arabs said "never," and vowed to annihilate the new Jewish state the moment the British withdrew.

Before we shift the lens of history from political to military events, let us first examine the dominant role also played by many American Jews in the establishment of the state of Israel. Among the many, tower three— Henrietta Szold (1860–1945), who brought American women into the Zionist movement with startling results; Rabbi Stephen S. Wise (1874– 1949), whose impassioned oratory swept the Zionist question into the White House of President Woodrow Wilson and the League of Nations; and Rabbi Abba Hillel Silver (1893–1963), whose magnetic oratory took the Zionist question into the White House of President Harry S. Truman and the United Nations.

Henrietta Szold, born in Baltimore, taught French, German, mathematics, and botany for fifteen years at a prestigious academy for girls in addition to teaching religion in her father's synagogue. Visiting Palestine in 1909, she was enthralled by that country's beauty but depressed by the misery of its people. Returning to the United States, she founded Hadassah which began organizing medical units of doctors and nurses to improve the health, medical care, and education of the people of Palestine. More than any other organization, Hadassah has been responsible for Israel's hygienic, medical, and health standards which today equal or exceed the standards of even the most advanced Western nations.

Rabbi Stephen S. Wise was known as the "first apostle to the Gentiles" because he was the first American Jew to take the cause of Zionism to Christian audiences. He was a formidable orator who could whip an audience into a frenzy of enthusiasm. He was so influential that the British consulted him on the formulation of the Balfour Declaration text.

In coordination with Louis D. Brandeis, the first Jewish justice of the Supreme Court, Wise made Zionism American. Together they laid the Zionist cause on the desk of President Woodrow Wilson. As a result, Wise, in December 1918, with a delegation of Zionists appointed by the president, headed for the peace talks at Versailles. At San Remo, Italy, where the conference on the homeland for the Jews in Palestine was held, the American delegation won and the Balfour Declaration was upheld. If not for that conference, the Balfour Declaration would have been a scrap of worthless paper, for the British were having second thoughts about it, now that World War I was won.

An equally crucial test for American Jewish statesmanship came after World War II, when the British mandate had to be converted into an independent Jewish state. That was the cue for the entry of Rabbi Abba Hillel Silver, a towering personality and chief American architect of Zionist policy from World War II until the founding of the state of Israel.

Silver was a passionate Zionist for whom Zionism and Judaism were one. When he thundered his Zionist gospel, it was heard throughout the land, from synagogues to the White House. He was instrumental in the passage of congressional resolutions favoring the Zionist cause and reached the height of his career when, in 1947, he presented the case for an independent Jewish state to the United Nations. And he was prominent among those who influenced President Harry S. Truman's decision to recognize the state of Israel.

Zionism had triumphed. Herzl had been vindicated. But now the mettle of the new state was to be tested on the battlefield.

35

The Age of
Heroism

On May 14, 1948, the world heard David Ben-Gurion, the first prime minister of the new state of Israel, declare its independence. On that day the British folded their tents, hauled down the Union Jack, and departed. And on that same day, five Arab armies invaded Israel.

The five wars that ensued could be compared to the succession of wars waged by Persia against Greece. But just as tiny Greece bested giant Persia, so tiny Israel—a country of but thirty thousand square miles with three million people—bested the giant Arab world with its combined land mass of 4,500,000 square miles* and 120 million people. These five wars have been named the War of Independence (1948), the Sinai Campaign (1956), the Six Day War (1967), the Yom Kippur War (1973) and the Lebanese War (1982).

The first conflict, the War of Independence, had an air of a Gilbert and Sullivan comic opera. Commanding the five invading Arab armies was a spit and polish model of a British officer—lieutenant general Sir John Bagot Glubb, Pascha, who issued a communique of victory before hostilities commenced.

The Arab high command gave a warning to the 650,000 Arabs in Israel to get out of the country in order to give the invading armies elbow room to annihilate the Jews, with the promise that they could return in a week to claim the homes and property of the slaughtered Jews. A half-million Arabs heeded the call. Those Arabs who stayed became Israeli citizens; those who left became the future refugees.

At first things looked bleak for the new Jewish state. Egyptian forces struck through the Gaza Strip, Jordanians seized Old Jerusalem threatening to cut Israel in two, and the Syrians poured in from the Golan Heights. Israel reeled under the blows.

*The United States encompasses only 3,000,000 square miles, including Hawaii and Alaska.

Then a miracle occurred. From the memory of their history, the Jews armed themselves with the shield of King David and the sword of Bar Kochba. Sir John Bagot Glubb, Pascha, ran into a wall of steel and guts. In bold, swift counterstrokes, the invaders were driven back. Instead of annihilating Israel, the Egyptians and Jordanians annihilated the Palestinian-Arab state which the United Nations had created. Egypt annexed the Gaza Strip, and Jordan grabbed the West Bank, the two component parts of the United Nations-sponsored Palestinian state. The Arabs lost the war against Israel. General Sir John Bagot Glubb, Pascha, was dismissed by the Arabs and pensioned off by the British.

Though the United Nations did nothing to prevent Egypt and Jordan from destroying the Arab-Palestinian state, it did prevent Israel from winning the peace. Encouraged by this intervention in their behalf, the Arab states refused to recognize Israel, and instead vowed a war of revenge.

Emboldened by help from Russia, Egypt in 1955 seized the Suez Canal from the French and British and, in 1956, Egypt poised her armies for a second strike at Israel.

Alert to the danger, Israel struck in the Gaza Strip and slashed across the Sinai. Within one hundred hours, Israel's army was strung along the Suez Canal from Port Said to Sharm el-Sheikh, ready to march on Cairo.

Now the war entered its international phase. The British and the French, either independently or in concert with Israel, had ringed Port Said with warships, bombed the town, and occupied. All seemed hopeless, when a miracle saved Egypt. The United States came to her aid.

Either fearful of an armed confrontation with Russia (as one version has it), or else irritated by the independent action of Jews, Frenchmen, and Englishmen (as another version goes), the United States pressured England and France into withdrawing their forces. Israel was left holding the bag.

The United States and Soviet Russia now pressured Israel to withdraw. And thus it came about that, instead of discussing peace, Egypt and her Arab allies prepared to fight a third time. Egypt demanded that the United Nations withdraw its peace-keeping forces so she could unleash the Egyptian tiger on Israel. The United Nations obliged.

On June 5, 1967, an Arab force of 650,000 men; 2,700 tanks; and 1,090 aircraft was unleashed against Israel. In six days it was all over. But instead of the smile being on the face of the Egyptian tiger it was on the faces of the Israeli victors. The world was stunned with admiration for Israel's brilliant victory.

Egypt, Syria, and Jordan screamed for the United Nations to stop this wanton Israeli victory, and the United Nations responded as predictably as Pavlov's dog. But this time Israel refused to evacuate the Sinai, Golan, West Bank, and Gaza Strip. Old Jerusalem, which had been reconquered from Jordan, was incorporated with New Jerusalem into one city—Jerusalem.

Encouraged by the support of the United Nations, and rearmed by the Russians, the Arabs prepared themselves for yet a fourth round of war. They struck on October 6, 1973, starting the Yom Kippur War, which almost cost Israel her existence.

It was 2:00 P.M., Yom Kippur; the entire nation was at prayer. Then, suddenly, heaven and earth erupted in horrid sound as bombs and shells exploded. This was the hour and day Egypt and Syria had chosen to invade Israel with a combined force of 800,000 men; 4,800 tanks; and 900 front line planes—more tanks than had been used by either Russians or Nazis in the great tank battle at Kursk in World War II.

Just as the United States was unprepared for the attack on Pearl Harbor, Israel, too, was unprepared for this invasion. At the crucial Bar Lev line which stretched along the Suez Canal for 105 miles, Israel had only 438 soldiers, three tanks, and seven artillery batteries.

Suddenly, before the astonished eyes of this small force there appeared tens of thousands of Egyptians, crossing along the entire length of the Suez Canal on anything that could float. By the end of the day, most of the Israeli defenders were dead. Thirty thousand Egyptians dug in on Israeli soil. Within a week the force grew to two-hundred thousand.

But Israel had a surprise for Egypt. Stashed twenty miles behind the Bar Lev line stood a tank division which she hurled at the Egyptians. Egypt, however, had an ever greater surprise for Israel. The division was met by a deadly barrage of new, hand-held, radar-guided, Russian-made Sagger rockets which could home in and annihilate a tank and its entire crew with one shot. Within an hour the Israeli tank division was annihilated.

The news from the Golan front was equally dismal. The Syrians were slashing their way across the Golan toward the Jordan Valley for a march on Jerusalem. By nightfall the Israeli lines were broken. The peril to Israel had never been greater.

Israel decided to concentrate its entire might on delivering the Syrians a post-Yom Kippur knockout punch. It was a grinding, remorseless fight, man against man, tank against tank, plane against plane—the survival of Israel against Syrian prestige. In the end Israeli grit won; the Syrians were hurled back to Damascus.

Israel now turned her fury on the Egyptians, avenging her previous defeat by decimating Egypt's main tank force.

By a stroke of luck, an Israeli advance unit stumbled upon a gap between the flanks of the two Egyptian armies along the Suez. Boldly, in the night, Israeli troops pushed without pause through that gap, across the Suez and into Egypt.

The Egyptians woke the next morning to behold the spectacle of Israeli soldiers on their soil, demolishing their missile batteries, destroying their tank depots, and marching toward Cairo, after having bottled up the two Egyptian armies in the Sinai like a twin fetus in a test tube. Egypt screamed for help.

Not a single Arab nation heard that cry, for none came to help. But Russia heard. She gave America an ultimatum—either order Israel to retreat to her 1967 borders, or Russia would send troops to Egypt to push Israel back.

President Richard Nixon, not one to take too kindly to a Russian ultimatum, ordered an alert of all American armed forces—land, sea, air, and atomic—throughout the world. Russia backed down and accepted the American plan which called for Israel not to annihilate the two Egyptian armies and to withdraw all her troops from Egyptian soil. Israel complied, and the Yom Kippur War was over.

And would you believe it? The cry was heard again: "Israel must withdraw to her 1967 borders," shouted the Arabs, "and then we will kill her." It was as if vanquished Nazi Germany and defeated Imperial Japan had demanded the right to dictate peace terms to the victorious allies in World War II. Not only was the situation ludicrous, it was obscene. Never before in history had victors been forced to beg the vanquished for peace.

After four years and no peace, one segment of Israeli society began to think that perhaps the best policy for Israel was to give in to the demands of the Arabs, retreat to the 1967 borders, and trust Arab goodwill. Another segment warned that surrender to the Arabs would mean the extinction of Israel. The time had come, they felt, to put an end by force to this deadly farce.

Was this a repetition of history—a repetition of the great debate in Jerusalem in 70 C.E. between the peace party and war party as to what course to take in the face of the Roman threat? Whose view should prevail—that of Johanan ben Zakkai advocating surrender, or that of Eleazar ben Yair counseling war.

The same debate had taken place in the 1930s with a different cast of characters. Which policy should the Western democracies have adopted vis-à-vis Nazi Germany—that of Neville Chamberlain's peace party advocating an accommodation with Hitler or that of Winston Churchill's war party counselling a stand against Hitler? In the words of Montaigne's epigram, "The more things change the more they remain the same."

This same debate is taking place in the United States today. What stand should the United States take vis-à-vis Russia? Should it be the Chamberlain line of accommodation or the Churchill line of standing up to the aggressor.

The answer depends upon the perception one has of the enemy. Then the responses are rationalized accordingly. Survival depends upon having the right perception and tailoring the response to it. History permits no second guessing.

After the Yom Kippur War, a new mood swept Israel. Menachem Begin, former head of the Irgun, was elected prime minister. For openers, he set the Arab world in turmoil with an announcement that the West Bank of the Jordan River was not occupied territory but Judea and Samaria, part of Israel itself. A second jolt to the Arabs came with his policy of increased Jewish settlements in Judea, Samaria, Golan, Gaza, Sinai.

Was Begin borrowing a page from American history? Wasn't that how the West was won? First came the settlers; then came the soldiers to protect them; and then came a request to be included in the Union. Were these new Israeli settlements preludes to annexations?

Whose land is Palestine anyhow?

There are three main arguments used in discussions on what belongs to whom: Who was there first? Who has been there the longest? Who won the war?

On the merits of the first argument, Israel is first by a big margin. The Jews got there first in 1,000 B.C.E. and the Arabs did not get there until 648 C.E.—1,600 years later.

The second argument is a numbers game. The answer depends on when one starts counting. In 800 B.C.E., the Jews were the majority in Palestine; in 800 C.E., it was the Arabs. In the twelfth century C.E., when the Christians had established the Latin kingdom in Palestine, the Christians were the majority. In 1947 C.E., it was the Arabs; in 1948 C.E., it was the Jews.

Thus far only the third argument—Who won the war?—has ever prevailed historically. The winner determines the verdict as to what belongs to whom. In history, the winning or losing of a war is not a moral judgment but a statement of fact. The Jews got Palestine by defeating the Canaanites and the Arabs got Palestine by defeating the Byzantines. The Crusaders lost Palestine to the Mameluks who lost it to the Turks, who lost it to the English who asked the United Nations to take over the headache. After the United Nations partitioned the country, the Arabs defied the United Nations and lost four times on the battlefield. And thus far the Jews have been able to hold on to their land against all aggressors.

Everyone predicted that the Arab response to the Jewish settlement of the West Bank would be a fifth war. To everyone's surprise, instead of war came the first Arab peace offer.

The first to divine the meaning of the new Israeli diplomacy was Egypt's President Anwar el-Sadat. Of all Arab countries, Egypt had paid the highest price for the four wars in men, money, and material. The other Arabs had always been willing to fight to the last Egyptian. Sadat wanted no more of it. He also realized he would not win back the Sinai on the battlefield and that the price of the Sinai would go up as Israeli settlements increased.

The time to strike a bargain over Sinai was now, while Prime Minister Begin was waiting for his first peace customer. Boldly, Sadat made his bid for peace and, equally boldly, Begin accepted. The two embraced before an astonished world; and with the cooperation of the United States, a peace treaty was hammered out.

Menachem Begin could now turn his attention to a new crisis developing in Lebanon. The Syrians had invaded Lebanon and installed Russian-made missiles on Lebanese soil but pointing at Israel. The Palestine Liberation Organization (P.L.O.)—a terrorist army subsidized by the Arabs and Russia—had also invaded Lebanon, and now almost a million Palestinians squatted in the land, terrorizing the Christian Lebanese population, while increasing deadly P.L.O. raids on Israel.

What should Israel do? Wait until she was again invaded and then defend herself, and be annihilated if she lost? Or make a preemptive strike against the P.L.O. and the Syrians?

Amidst great controversy, Begin made the decision that it was time for Israel to make the omelette instead of again being one. If the Arabs wanted a total war of the entire Arab world against Israel, so be it. Begin felt that Israel had to take a stand, she could not survive an indefinite series of wars forever.

Swiftly, Israel's army slashed deeply into Lebanon. The Christian Lebanese hailed them as liberators. In quick succession the Syrian missile sites were obliterated; Russian planes were shot down from the sky like pheasants in season and the P.L.O. was routed from its strongholds in Southern Lebanon.

The world press warned Israel not to move further north; that if it dared march on Beirut, every Arab country would declare war on Israel and that Russia would intervene. Israeli forces marched north and routed the P.L.O. from Beirut.

Not a single Arab country came to the aid of the P.L.O. or Syria. Russia stayed out, content to issue a few abusive missives but no missiles. The P.L.O. was forced to evacuate Beirut. The United States, however, stopped the war before Israel had time to drive out the Syrians.

The Lebanese War is still too close to our times for history to judge its effect. But some results can be assessed. Though the war did not make the Arabs love Israel any more than they had, it did force them to reassess how much their hate had cost them, and how absurd the wars had been. Even more important, the Arab states began to realize that the longer they postponed a valid peace, the higher the price would be in the future.

Israel prays for peace. But as in the days of Ezra and Nehemiah the people are rebuilding Israel with a trowel in one hand and a sword in the other, ready for either peace or war.

36
A Touch of the Future

Even more amazing than her victories on the battlefield against incredible odds, are Israel's victories in the field of social achievement. She is the only country born in the aftermath of World War II that has achieved a standard of democracy and groceries equal to that of the most advanced nations in the Western world

In 1900, after twenty centuries of exploitation by a succession of invaders (Romans, Byzantines, Arabs, Christians, Mamluks, and Turks), Palestine had become a poverty-stricken province in the Ottoman empire, barely able to support 150,000 people. Fifty years later, after the arrival of the first Zionists, Israel became a modern agricultural and industrial state supporting over four million people.

Since her independence in 1948, the original 650,000 Jews in Israel have ingathered more than three million Jewish immigrants from all over the world, quintupling her population. Within one generation, Israel integrated them all into one proud nation.

From its very inception as a state, even as the War of Independence was being fought, Israel laid the foundation for a nation based on the Mosaic concept of equality with justice for all. No Jew anywhere in the world needed to pass a means test to become an Israeli citizen. All a Jew had to do was to land in Israel and openly declare that he or she wanted to become a citizen of the country.

The franchise, universal education, and the right to hold a job in accordance with one's ability was granted to all, irrespective of race, creed, color, sex, or previous condition of servitude. For the first time in history, Arab women could vote, a privilege no Arab woman has in any Arab country.

In the academic world, Israel created one miracle after another. The Hebrew University of Jerusalem, founded in 1920, already vies in academic honors with Harvard, Oxford, and the Sorbonne. The Weizmann Institute of Science has become world famed for its innovations and discoveries. The Technion in Haifa is famed for its pioneering in agricultural and aeronautical engineering and in chemical technology.

As the country grew, so grew the number of schools, theaters, museums, symphony halls. Israel has more bookstores and art galleries per capita than any other nation in the world. Its infant mortality is the lowest in the world; its literacy rate among the highest, despite the fact the majority of its population is not as yet native born. The joke in Israel is that it is the only country in the world where children teach parents the native tongue, for the children grow up with Hebrew whereas many parents have to learn it.

In Israel, four thousand years of history look down every day upon citizens and tourists. But Israel is also a touch of the future. In spite of all technological advances, the Jewish people still have a vision of the messianic ideal—the redemption of the Jews through the soil of Israel. No philosophy, no logic, no science has altered this Jewish belief in a prophetic manifest destiny. The distant past is closer to the heart of the Jew than recent history. Nothing—not anti-semitism, not fascism, not communism—can uproot this attachment of the Jews to their past history, or blind their vision of the future.

The Prophets were the first to call upon the Jews to enter world history as a prototype of an ethical world community and to be an example for mankind. Is Jerusalem, now the spiritual homeland for Diaspora Jews, destined to become the spiritual world capital for all mankind? Is the Judaism of the Prophets destined to become a universal creed for the universal man of the future? In the words of Isaiah: "For out of Zion shall go forth the Law and the Word of the Lord from Jerusalem."

After two thousand and five hundred years, Isaiah's words still express the longing of human beings of all faiths, the universal hope of mankind.

We have now traversed four thousand years of history—from Abraham, the first Jew, to Ben-Gurion, the first prime minister of the new Jewish state.

We saw Jewish history begin with a handful of Hebrews wandering around the Mesopotamian world. Today there are over fifteen million Jews—four million in Israel and eleven million in the Diaspora. During their four-thousand-year odyssey they have visited practically every civilization and now reside in all five continents. Could we now perhaps paraphrase the words of Isaiah thus: From Zion shall go forth the Law and in the Diaspora it shall reach all mankind.

Though we have come to the end of the Second Act, we have not come to the end of Jewish history. There is yet a Third Act to come—another two thousand years with new challenges and more exciting adventures for the Jews.

Jews have given the world God, Abraham, Moses, Isaiah, Jesus, Spinoza, Marx, Freud, Einstein. They have given the world the Torah, the Prophets, democracy, Christianity, Mohammedanism, socialism—even theoretial physics. These are the idea governing two-thirds of the world today. Who else has a track record like this?

You are members of a team of winners!

If you don't believe it, ask yourself, Where are all the others who started out with the Jews forty centuries ago?

However, at this point we must issue a word of caution. Thus far the Jews have seemed indestructible. But their indestructibility does not spring from any innate Jewish physical or mental qualities. What has given the Jews their indestructibility has been their ideas stemming from the Torah. It is these ideas that are indestructible, and the Jews with them. The moment the Jews forsake these ideas, they become as destructible as any other people.

The message is clear: If the Jews want to remain indestructible, for the sake of Jews, God, and History, they must hold on to those ideas; they must not give up now.

Index

D. BLUESTEIN